Called To Be HIS SERVANT

Barbed Wire Interlude

H.C. Kiser, Jr.

A Biography by Beverly Harding-Mullins

CALLED TO
BE HIS SERVANT

H.C. KISER, JR.

CALLED TO
BE HIS SERVANT

H.C. KISER, JR.

A biography by Beverly Harding-Mullins

Credits:
Cover and graphic design by Myra Windle Danehy.
Cover photograph by Larry Dean.
Back cover photograph by Betty Moser.

Called To Be His Servant, H.C. Kiser, Jr.
by Beverly Harding-Mullins.

All Scripture quotations, unless otherwise indicated, are taken from the *Holy Bible, New International Version®. NIV®.* Copyright ©1973, 1978, 1984 by International Bible Society. Used by permission of Zondervan Publishing House. All rights reserved.

Some Scripture quotations in this book are taken from the *NEW AMERICAN STANDARD BIBLE®,* © Copyright The Lockman Foundation 1960, 1962, 1963, 1971, 1972, 1973, 1975, 1977. Used by permission.

Verses marked LB are taken from *The Living Bible* ©1971. Used by permission of Tyndale House Publishers, Inc. Wheaton, IL 60189. All rights reserved.

Verses marked KJV are taken from *The King James* version of the Bible.

Sanctuary. Copyright 1982. *Whole Armor / Full Armor Publishing.* Administered by **The Kruger Organisation, Inc.** 15 Rolling Way, New City, NY, 10956-6912. International Copyright Secured. All rights reserved. Used by permission.

Library of Congress Catalog Card Number: 98-93104

ISBN: 0-9664511-0-4

Printed in the United States of America

*Let your conversation be without
covetousness; and be content with
such things as ye have: for he
hath said, I will never leave thee,
nor forsake thee.*

(HEBREWS 13:5, KJV)

Contents

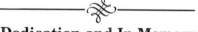

Dedication and In Memory

This book is dedicated to Ed Sutherland, who gave me encouragement and helped me to regain some esteem and confidence after I returned home from being a POW in Germany in World War II. Ed kept encouraging me and often said, "You can do it, keep trying." Ed helped me get my first job after I came home, and I would ride to work with him.

In loving memory of my parents, Dacy and Hiram Kiser, Sr.; my grandfather, Elihu Kiser, whose Christian life and his walk with Christ made me want to become a Christian and walk in his steps; also, Granny Woolwine, who so many times said, "Son, you ought to put this story in writing."

H. C. Kiser Jr.

Dedication

I would like to dedicate this book to my dad Bill Dingus. May God be glorified and honored!

Beverly

ACKNOWLEDGMENTS

As I look back over my life, I have so many joyful memories; but most precious to me are the people who have been so much inspiration and encouragement to me. Some of the people are named in this book, but a far greater number are not. I praise God for them!

I want especially to thank my wife Grace; my children Cindy, Fred, Mike, and Zan; and my grandsons Kyle, Evan, and Austin for their love and support. Also, I thank the people at my church, Abingdon Baptist, who never ceased to pray for me while I was a POW.

The other person I am grateful to is Beverly Mullins. She has spent countless hours typing and compiling information. She has brought to this project the qualities and technical skills so critical in producing a book. She has an eye for details and accuracy, probing me with questions that made me think. Most of all, I am grateful to her for seeking the guidance of the Holy Spirit. How grateful I am that Christ chose her to put the book together.

First, and last, I thank Jesus Christ who promised "He would never leave me, nor forsake me;" I give Him all the credit. My prayer is that God will receive all of the glory and praise that He truly deserves. I am thankful that He has chosen me to become a servant of His, which is a great calling.

H.C. Kiser, Jr.

ACKNOWLEDGMENTS

I want to express my heartfelt thanks to the following for their contributions in the assembly of this book:

Jack Garland, Ph. D.
Kellie Crowe
Lisa Campbell
Loretta Cox
Dale Winship
Garrett Sheldon, Ph. D.
Bill Whittaker, D. Min.
Randy Smith
Hilda Padgett
Ray and Dana Duncan
Preston and Yvonne Brown
Shayne Crenshaw
Rev. Carl Young
Don Moore
Tom Deaton
Juls and Barbara Wood

Jerry Peaks
Jim Johnson
Ann Colley
Betty Fritz
Matthew and Pearl Creel
John Daniels
Rev. Michael Somers
Bruce Hicks
Dr. Larry Pace, Jr.
Harry Gunter
John Gray
Shawn Elledge
Don Farmer
John Yeatts
Leander and June Roberts
Farris Funeral Home

I am so grateful to my husband Mike and our children Christy, Kyle, and Rachel for their patience, understanding, and encouragement. There are many others who have been so gracious with their love, support, and prayers. I have been blessed and delighted by the many people who have been willing to give their time to talk with me about H.C. and his impact on their lives.

Thank you and God bless you!

Beverly Harding-Mullins

QUIET MAN

A beacon light
    shining softly
        in the long dark
A warm breeze
    sheltering our spirit
        from the bitter wind
A quiet man
    living his life
        for the Good Lord
Sharing his love
    with all in need
        of hope
The grace of God
    a gift to all
        who will accept it
My life is better
    because of your life
My faith is stronger
        because of your faith
Thank you, quiet man
        the sermon is preached
Without a word
    the lesson is taught
        by example
Thank you, quiet man
    for sharing your life
        with mine.

For H.C.
December 3, 1995

Randall W. Smith

INTRODUCTION

Today we live in a hard-driving, rights-centered world. Kind consideration seems almost out of place. People are fearful of reaching out to others; but, as Christians, it is always appropriate, and it can deliver a powerful witness. One such servant is H.C. Kiser, Jr., a quiet man whose witness speaks louder than great waves crashing onto the shore. He is a hardworking, family man who loves the Lord with all of his heart, and who allows the Lord to be first and foremost in his life. He never has to speak a word; his demeanor speaks of Christ—Christ today in an ordinary man. Not a perfect man, but a man with his eyes focused on Jesus.

H.C.'s faith has been refined by fire. "Though now for a little while, [he] may have had to suffer grief in all kinds of trials, these have come to [him] so that [his] faith - of greater worth than gold, which perishes even though refined by fire - may be proved genuine, and may result in praise, glory, and honor when Jesus Christ is revealed" (1 Peter 1:6-7, NIV). H.C. has come full circle. His life began living and working on his family's farm in Washington County, Virginia. The desire of his heart is to put into words his walk with Jesus. This is how he sees his life; he has never been alone. We all know trials and tribulations; H.C. gives God all of the credit for victory over death and misery. H.C. has seen that Jesus IS life. Jesus walked with H.C. on Germany's "Death March"; Jesus looked at H.C. from his mirror as he prepared to go for his cancer treatment. Today, Jesus walks with H.C. as he continues to live and work on the farm.

H.C. is God's servant. H.C. always has a kind word and a peaceful, knowing smile for everyone. In John 16:33, NIV, Jesus said, "In this world, you will have trouble. But take heart! I have overcome the world." One senses the Lord saying this through H.C.'s look and mannerisms. When I or anyone else has said this to H.C., he humbly lowers his head. I know the Lord will smile that same peaceful smile at H.C. and say, "Well done, good and faithful servant" (Matthew 25:21, NIV).

I thank God for the opportunity to put into words this life of servanthood, so that God can speak to others of His love, His peace, and His joy. This isn't a story about a miracle or a tale of one incident; this is a life of servanthood, a life allowing the Holy Spirit to live in a German concentration camp, in Tanzania, in a crisis in South Carolina, in a small town called Abingdon, Virginia, and now in your home. Praise God, and may He be glorified by these written words. H.C., there are no words to describe my love and appreciation.

Your Friend In Christ,

Beverly

Chapter 1

H.C. KISER, JR.

You are our letter, written in our hearts, known and read by all men; being manifested that you are a letter of Christ, cared for by us, written not with ink, but with the Spirit of the living God, not on tablets of stone, but on tablets of human hearts. And such confidence we have through Christ toward God. Not that we are adequate in ourselves to consider anything as coming from ourselves, but our adequacy is from God.

(2 CORINTHIANS 3:2-5, NASB)

"Jesus, why do you love me so much that you didn't let me die? I can't wait to ask the Lord HOW I made it through that time!" H.C. and I are sitting at his kitchen table, and Grace, his wife of more than 50 years is bustling around in the kitchen preparing lunch. H.C. Kiser, Jr., is telling me about his walk with Jesus. Even he is still so amazed at the incredible love of Christ he has known during his 72 years as he recalls the events and miracles of his life. Reciting, almost word for word, Psalm 30 from the Living Bible, he becomes so excited that even being around him, the Spirit is contagious. "I will praise You Lord, for you have saved me from my enemies" (Psalm 30:1, LB).

Enemies? That time? The enemy and the time could be when, at 29,000 feet, the B-17 that H.C. was on was hit by a burst of flak from the huge 88 mm. cannons below in war-torn Bologna, Italy. The concussion from the burst stopped the forward motion of the plane, and a crushing force propelled the entire crew to the top of the plane as it went into a sharp dive.

The enemy and the time could be the horror he endured in the German prison camp where he was starved and beaten, shot at, threatened, and ridiculed. H.C. asks, "How did I endure? Literally, Jesus must have physically carried me through many days, many days that I can't even bring to consciousness. I can't wait to sit and talk with Jesus and praise Him for that time."

The enemy and the time could be when he had settled into the routine horror of a German prison camp and is then told they are leaving. The Russian army is getting closer, and they must move. Fifteen thousand starving men are marched the hundred miles from Nuremberg to Moosburg. No man could be prepared for the Death March. H.C. stood with his feet completely frozen, his own body waste freezing to him as it ran down his legs. H.C. stares, realizing in horror that they must leave behind literally hundreds of men huddled into the fetal

HC in dress uniform.
Photograph taken in February 1946

Entered Service:
April 7, 1943.
Branch:
Army Air Force
Trained:
Miami Beach, Florida
Amarillo, Texas,
Kingman, Arizona,
Dyersburg, Tennessee
Embarkation:
August 9, 1944
Returned:
June 5, 1945
Theatre of operations:
European-African-Middle Eastern
Rank:
Technical Sergeant

Engagements:
Rome-Arno, North Apennines, Po Valley, Southern France, Rhineland, Central Europe, Balkans
Awarded:
Seven Battle Stars, Air Medal with Cluster, Air Crew Member Wings
Discharged:
Maxwell Field, Alabama; October 21, 1945

position as they lay frozen to death or dying in the field. He is ordered to march on. He stands his frozen jacket against a tree and turns to leave.

The enemy and the time could be in 1972 when he grabbed the doorknob preparing to leave for his cancer treatment, and Christ reminded him of his prayer 28 years earlier. Gripping the door latch to prepare to jump from a burning B-17 with a mass of tangled parachute, H.C. prayed, "Lord, I don't know what to do, but I just pray that you will help me make the right decision: should I bail out or should I ride this burning bomber down?" The Lord said, "H.C., I am a God of miracles;

3

and if you'll just leap out into space with a torn parachute, I will show you that I am a God of miracles."

What is so unique about this man? Nothing. He is an ordinary man, a man who has given his life to Christ; therefore, not ordinary. Ask H.C., "Are you special? Are you better than anyone else?" His answer: "No, I am constantly seeking Jesus; I have so much to learn, so much I want to know!" He reflects a genuine humility that comes only from Jesus. There are no doubts that Jesus is speaking to you, teaching you, loving you.

Dr. Lawrence Pace, Jr., a former pastor of Abingdon Baptist Church, recalls a woman telling him of the time when her husband had heard H.C.'s testimony, and how it changed his life. Though a Christian, her husband had never realized the Lord is with us in times of difficulty and trials. He said, "I knew it in my head, but not in my heart. When H.C. was recalling all of the things he had been through, he was sharing more than those events: he was sharing how the Lord was with him through it all, and I felt the Lord's presence. I had been wondering why the Lord wasn't doing something to get me out of my problems. H.C. made me realize that the Lord wasn't taking me out of them; He was there with me."

Chapter 2

A Firm Foundation

*He is like a man building
a house, who dug deep and laid
a foundation upon the rock; and
when a flood rose, the torrent
burst against that house and
could not shake it, because it had
been well built.*

(Luke 6:48, NASB)

H.C. considers himself very fortunate having been raised in a Christian home. His family would have a family altar or prayer time together. It would seem to H.C. that his grandfather would wait until he was out in the yard playing with a bunch of his friends; then, he would holler outside and say it was time to come in for prayer. At the time, H.C. would be almost embarrassed. But now looking back, he is glad he did it and very grateful for a loving and Godly family. When he was growing up, his grandparents, Elihu and Priscilla Kiser, lived in the home with H.C. and his parents, Hiram Clay and Dacy Katherine Kiser, and his sister Ann.

Hiram Clay Kiser, Sr., known as "Hi," and Dacy courting. Photographed on the mountain in Chaney Creek.

H.C. was born on February 17, 1924 on Chaney Creek, which is in the mountains of Southwest Virginia in Russell County. There are two mining towns fairly close: Dante and Wilder. His sister Ann tells that when their mother went into labor with H.C., their father had to walk from Chaney Creek to where the doctor, R.L. Hillman, lived in Wilder. Hiram, Sr., better known as "Hi," had to cross the mountain to get to the doctor. The doctor's wife was

Dacy Kiser's family. Dacy's maiden name was Kiser and she married a Kiser. Photographed in front of the home of Chaney Creek built by Elihu Kiser. All ornate work was handcrafted.

Left to Right:
front row-Dacy, Frona,
Dora, mother Priscilla;
back row- Jake,
Luther, father Elihu.

in labor the same night and also delivered a son. Mrs. Kiser had a difficult delivery and lost quite a lot of blood. The doctor stayed with Mrs. Kiser through the night even though his own child was being born. H.C. says that he can't remember much about those early days, but he knows he had a loving family. His family attended Mt. Zion Baptist Church. Since they had a visiting preacher that only came ever so often, they didn't have

Hiram Clay Kiser, Sr. and Dacy Kiser. Photographed at a studio in Bluefield, Virginia.

This photograph was taken in 1925 at the old home on Chaney Creek.H.C.'s grandmother Priscilla and his mother Dacy would prepare Sunday dinner for this family gathering. Often, twice this many would join the family for dinner after church services.

Left to Right: front row- Ralph Kiser, Ruth Kiser, Claude Kiser, Dana Amburgey, Nell Carter, Lenora Amburgey, Charlie Carter, Elva Carter, Lance Kiser, Ann Kiser, Virginia Patton; second row- Maude Kiser, Luther Kiser, Pauline Kiser, Estelle Amgurgey, Clyde Carter, Lawrence Pearce, Curt Amburgey, Dacy Kiser, H.C. Kiser (in arms), Frona Amburgey, Dora Patton, W.C. Patton (in arms); third row- Jake Kiser, Jessie Ruth Kiser (in arms), Elihu Kiser, Priscilla Kiser, Will Carter, Tacy Carter, Jack Carter (in arms), Hiram Kiser, Ritt Kiser.

services every Sunday. When the church had gatherings, everyone would say, "Let's go to Uncle Elihu's for dinner." H.C.'s mother and grandmother would feed as many as 60 people on a Sunday; H.C. still wonders how they did it. They had no refrigeration, but they had a well house and a dairy. His grandfather always had a large garden and grew many things that he peddled. Elihu had bees, and he carried the honey on horseback to town to sell when he took it off the hives. He was a logger, and he also worked in the mines for a short time.

H.C. was around five when his family moved to Abingdon, Virginia. His grandmother died about this time, and his grandfather continued to live with them until his death in 1951. Grandpa Elihu was a very strict person. H.C. said, "We had better do whatever he said." He didn't interfere with what H.C.'s parents said, but he had his own beliefs and expectations for H.C. and Ann.

H.C.'s grandfather would take him out into the fields of the family farm with him. When they would have a little break, he would talk to H.C. about the Lord. Elihu called H.C. "Buddy." He would say, "Buddy, growing up in a Christian home does not make you a Christian. You need to accept Jesus as your Lord and Savior."

The family did not have a car so they walked to church. They attended Spring Creek Presbyterian Church for a while; but in the mid-to later 1930's, they started going to Abingdon Baptist Church. H.C. had a Godly mother and father. His father, a great teacher of the Bible, taught the Men's Bible Class. Asked about anything, he could always find it in the Bible. He was a man of deep conviction and sincerity; he had great faith and knowledge of the Bible. He worded beautiful prayers and was a very eloquent speaker and writer, though he never went beyond the eighth grade in school. H.C.'s grandfather never went to school; he was self-taught. He was a great reader and writer. He used to write columns for the local Lebanon News, the Lebanon, Virginia, weekly newspaper. He was never ordained as a minister, but he conducted funerals. He never studied music, but he could play hymns on the piano and sing beautifully. On Sunday nights, the family would always listen to preachers on the radio. There was always a sermon, and H.C. and Ann had to sit as though they were in church. They couldn't laugh or talk, they had to sit still quietly and listen. There would be a big fire in the fireplace, and they would pop corn and sit around the fireplace eating popcorn and listening to the Sunday night service.

H.C. went to a little one-room school called Spring Creek School, which offered the first five grades of elementary school. He and Ann walked to school through a pasture field of grazing sheep, and there was always this one buck sheep which they were afraid of. On more than one occasion, when they had reached the field on their way home, they would see the big buck and walk all the way back to school and go around the road via Route 11 to their home. H.C. went to Cleveland High School for one year. Then, he rode the bus to William King High School so that he could play sports. After he graduated, he went to Washington County Technical School to take a course in Auto Mechanics.

Ann and H.C. as children photographed on Chaney Creek, ages six and four respectively.

H.C. grew up during the Depression; but having grown up on a farm, he says that he didn't realize there was a Depression. Since they grew everything on the farm, they had their own produce and meat. They had milk cows, which H.C. and Ann drove in from the fields and helped milk. They had hogs, and H.C.'s mother raised chickens and turkeys. She would take them to a produce house and buy sugar and coffee and the other few staples they couldn't grow on the farm. When it was harvest time, his family had lots of corn and wheat. H.C.'s father and grandfather would bring in big bags of corn, and H.C. and Ann would sit in front of the fireplace and shell the corn. After the wheat was threshed, they would take the wheat and corn by wagon to Abingdon to the mill where it was ground into meal and flour. Their home didn't have centralized heat then; and since the upstairs was away from the fireplace and cold, they would put the flour and meal upstairs in Grandpa's room. They had horses which H.C. and Ann would ride bareback. The horses were used instead of tractors to do the plowing and cultivating.

Growing up on the farm, H.C. and Ann always had chores to do. They were expected to do them; they didn't argue about it because they knew everyone had a part to do. At first, it was carrying in the kindling and coal. Their father would carry in the big logs because they couldn't manage them. They used a coal-and-wood cook stove. His parents had a big fancy stove called a Heatrola in the living room. The stovepipe went into the chimney of a big fireplace. Stoking the Heatrola was just another one of their chores. As they got older, they had to help with the more difficult work on the farm—setting and suckering tobacco. They didn't spray it then to kill the suckers; they had to go through the patch and break them out.

H.C.'s family and those around them had plenty of food, but there were people passing through the area who would come to his family's door and ask for food. His mother always fed them. At that time, Route 11 was the main highway in the area; and sometimes when H.C.'s grandfather was working in the garden, a traveler might "holler up" and ask for a drink of water or something. His mother would take the traveler in and feed him; and before that person got back on the road, his grandfather would share Christ with him. H.C. says his grandfather never missed an opportunity to witness to anyone — to speak about Jesus Christ. His grandfather had a lot of influence in H.C.'s life. H.C. had decided to join the Service; and as time approached, he wanted to make his life right with the Lord. H.C. accepted Jesus Christ as his Savior at Abingdon Baptist Church. Reverend Paul Roberts was the evangelist, and he prayed with H.C. in a little inquiry room upstairs in the church.

H.C. at Basic Training Center #9, Miami Beach Florida, June 1943

Chapter 3

VOLUNTEERING FOR THE ARMY AIR FORCE

Trust in the Lord with all your heart, And do not lean on your own understanding; in all your ways acknowledge him and he will make your paths straight.

(PROVERBS 3:5,6, NIV)

H.C. at age nineteen. Photo taken at aerial gunnery school, Kingman Army Air Field, Kingman, Arizona

H.C. volunteered for the U.S. Army Air Force when he was 19. He knew that he would be drafted and decided to go ahead and sign up. One day, before he was to leave for training, H.C. was standing on a hilly place on the farm and looked out over the land he loved. He thought of growing up, working, and playing on the farm. His heart was filled with a heavy burden about the future. H.C. said, "I felt kind of like Solomon did when he said in 1 Kings 3:7, NASB, 'I am but a little child; I do not know how to go out or come in.' I thought of all of the uncertainties that lay ahead: what I would do with my life, who I would marry — I had so many questions. I just left them, and did the best I knew, I turned them over to the Lord. I invited Him to take over my life and help me in every aspect, in every decision I would make. Proverbs 3:5,6, NIV, says 'Trust in the Lord with all your heart and lean not on your own understanding; in all your ways acknowledge Him, and He will make your paths straight.' I felt a desperate need to seek Christ with all of my heart. I made a vow to the Lord that I would trust Him to protect me and bring me home. He gave me assurance that sooner or later I would return to the farm.

We made a covenant. As Jacob had wrestled with the angel, he told the Lord he wouldn't live without going back as a servant to God. I, too, wanted to live; I, too, wanted to survive the wrath of war. I wanted to

14

return to the farm — the land, and I vowed to the Lord to return as His servant. I would witness at every opportunity. I can still go to that same hilly place on the farm, and I remember the promise that I made; I remember that God brought me through many trials and hardships, that He saved me by His grace, and I have given my life to the Lord. I want to tell as many people as I can about Jesus and all of the miracles He has wrought in my life."

H.C. and Grace Hutton had been "courting" and attending church together for several years. On the night before H.C. left for basic training, he had gone to visit with Grace. H.C. says that when he was leaving, he thought he might never see her again so he wanted to give her a good-bye kiss. He said, "I was so nervous and excited that after I kissed her, I turned to leave; and I walked off the porch and fell right into the middle of a rose bush. I just jumped up and walked away; I didn't feel a thing!"

H.C. left Abingdon on April 14, 1943. There were 40 young men who left by train that day. Irene Cardwell, a high school friend, had signed H.C. up for the Army Air Corps. She had told H.C. to take the paperwork along, and she assigned him Corporal and put him in charge of the train coach. He was in charge of the men until they got to Camp Lee, Virginia. They had just gotten started on the train when a friend of his had a toothache. The friend had a bottle of liquor, and he got drunk and vomited all over the coach. When they arrived at Camp Lee, the Sergeant started, "All right, who has the papers, who's in charge?" He chastised H.C. for the incident. He was at Camp Lee for a while and was then sent to Miami Beach, Florida, for basic training.

He was sent to Amarillo, Texas, for aircraft mechanic's school. In mechanic's school he studied all of the functions of the B-17 bomber. The Air Corps asked him if he would like to specialize on one phase of the B-17. They were supposed to send him to Wichita Falls to be a specialist on hydraulic systems. They asked him if he wanted to fly combat, and he said, "No." About halfway through aircraft mechanic's school in Amarillo, he was given a physical, pulled out of the school, and sent to Kingman, Arizona, to aerial gunner's school. H.C. said, "I told you I didn't want to fly combat." It didn't make any difference if he wanted to or not, he did it.

From Amarillo, Texas, H.C. was sent to Kingman Army Air Force base, and from there to Dyersburg,

Tennessee. It was at Dyersburg where he met the crew of the plane he would be assigned to. During training flights they would go up, circle the base, "bomb" landings, and come back. There were bomb runs along the Mississippi River, and the crew had artificial targets to aim for. They used sacks of lime that looked like bombs, and the bombardiers would practice high altitude bombing through clouds.

H.C. in flying gear in Lincoln, Nebraska. Waiting to be assigned to his regular crew.

H.C. and the

crew left Dyersburg and went to Lincoln, Nebraska. They would practice as a crew going from there to New Orleans, Louisiana, and drop "bombs" on a football stadium or other unusual target. H.C. says they would fly hundreds of miles and go to Cleveland, Ohio, and "bomb" automobile factories. They would fly for hours and hours just to check the bombardier and the navigator and for the pilot to see how the crew was going to respond. The navigator, Lt. Miller, kept getting them lost, and the only saving maneuver would be to come to the Mississippi River, which would give them a bearing. Then they would know to go north or south because the base was right along the Mississippi River.

The crew went from Lincoln to Kearney, Nebraska, where they picked up the B-17 Flying Fortress. They took it and had the markings put on the tail. H.C. said they were all so proud of it. The crew flew to Labrador and from there they took off for the Azore Islands. The B-17 had just enough fuel to get to the Azore Islands. If they missed it, they would be in big trouble because there was a certain area there where radio contact with the United States was lost. The crew was depending on the navigator. H.C. said they told him they were going to throw him out if he didn't get them right on target. He hit the target area straight on, and they refueled in the Azores. They flew over North Africa and from there went to Foggia, Italy. H.C. was stationed out of Foggia Air Base, which housed the 463rd Bomb group and all the different squadrons. H.C. was in the 772nd Squadron and attached to the 15th Air Force.

H. C. was 19 years old. He had left the family farm to go to war. When he left, he wasn't sure where he would end up or what he would be doing. But, as the army trained and moved him from state to state and finally to Foggia, Italy, H.C. began to realize the importance of a personal relationship with Jesus.

This is evident from the following excerpts from letters H.C. wrote to his mother in late 1943 and early 1944:

> *It seems like a fellow does go to church (in the army), every chance that he gets and just for one reason only. Sometimes back home we may have gone just to showoff some new clothes, or to listen to the choir (and criticize the preacher) ha. You know that I could think of a lot of reasons for going to church at home, but I go here just for the good that I can derive from going.*
> **Dec. 10, 1943 from Amarillo Army Air Field, Amarillo, Texas.**

> *Well, I went to church this morning at the 11:00 a.m. service. It reminded me of being at home for church for it was the first time that I had gotten off for the 11:00 service in a long time. The chaplain talked pretty good, he used one of Paul's statements for his text which says that all things work together for good to them that trust the Lord. So I figure that things will turn out for the best in the long run. After all mom, you know with all the promises and assurances that the Lord has given us of the better days ahead! Well, it just doesn't leave "even a soldier" much room for worrying.*
> **January 16, 1944 from Amarillo Army Air Field, Amarillo, Texas.**

> *Well you know a fellow in the army doesn't get to attend or listen to good sermons like he had in civilian life, although I know that I am more interested in my spiritual life now than I was at home. I'm pretty sure too that these ten months that I've had in the army would have been pretty tough, if I hadn't have had the faith and hopes that always help out when the going*

gets tough. Then besides, I wouldn't attempt this aerial gunnery course on my own strength, but I'm sure that I can make it since I'll have the Lord along to help when the going gets too rough for me to handle. You know that a gunner or an entire crew is foolish if they rely on themselves. Well I didn't mean to preach a Sunday sermon, but I just wanted to let you know how I stand on this gunnery situation. So, mom, I don't see where you folks can find any room for worrying about me.

February 6, 1944 from Kingman Army Air Field, Kingman, Arizona.

By-the-way mom here's something else that I know you all will be glad to know. Well before we take off for a mission the pilot discusses the target and he also informs us as to the number of enemy fighters we're supposed to meet and their location, etc. Then last of all but not <u>least</u> we always get into a little huddle, all hugged up, (like a football team) and then after removing our helmets some member of the crew (usually the pilot) leads us in prayer. Boy we're really lucky to have a guy like that for a pilot for I don't know of another crew that takes time to say a little prayer before the mission. It's surprising to how much that helps and the courage that it brings is always sufficient for even the roughest mission.

I just wanted to let you know this mom so you know that we're in "safekeeping" and I think its a lot of nonsense for either of you folks or me either to do any worrying. Isn't that right?? I don't think the Germans have a big enough cannon to knock down our Fort anyway.

Excerpt of letter written on August 28, 1944, by H.C. to his mother. Photograph of actual letter on next page.

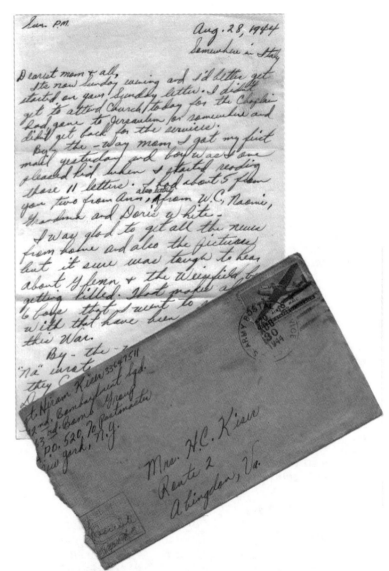

This letter was written from "somewhere in Italy." H.C. wanted his mother to know the crew was placing their lives in God's "safekeeping."

K-949 Weapons Department
Kingman Army Air Field, Kingman, Arizona

SUBJECT: An Important Message.
TO: All New Gunnery Students.

You men are now entering your first academic phase in gunnery. You will find that it is one of the most important courses you will have in this school. The instructors are capable and realize that if they let down at any time it may cost a gunner his life. So if you cooperate just a little the course will be easy and interesting. The school realizes that some of you do not want to be gunners but know that you are an American, and it is the American way to do anything that you are best qualified for. All of the instructors feel that the gunner is the most important man on a combat crew. A B-17 or B-29 is just as powerful as its worst gunner. You men, once you have attained a pair of wings become one of the chosen few. You are respected everywhere you go. This you will deserve as your life is no easy one. You have a job to do and we know you will do it and do it damn well. You see, we know Americans.

While you are in this school there are rules that must be obeyed. To be able to give orders you must be able to take them. It is known that you will graduate only as PFC and Corporal, but it has also been proven that a good gunner never goes into combat with less than a Buck Sergeants rating. The following rules must be obeyed or you will be on the labor detail on Sunday. Sunday is your only day off and it is very nice to rest at that time so be wise and follow orders.

Part of the captain's speech given to new gunnery students at Kingman Army Air Field, Kingman, Arizona, February 1944.

Chapter 4

SHOT DOWN

Dear Friends, do not be surprised at the painful trial you are suffering, as though something strange were happening to you. But rejoice that you participate in the sufferings of Christ, so that you may be overjoyed when his glory is revealed.

(1 PETER 4:12,13, NIV)

H.C. was an aerial gunner on a B-17 Bomber crew. The famous B-17 Bomber has had much recognition as a combat aircraft, much more than any military aircraft of World War II. The plane had a crew of ten men; the regular pilot was Irvin Kipper. The crew named the flying fortress, *Pretty Gertie*, after Kipper's wife Gertrude. He was the only member of the crew who was married. The co-pilot was James Crow. Douglas Johnson was the right waist gunner and H.C. was the left waist gunner. David Miller was the navigator. Phillip Daily was the tail gunner. Fedoro DeTunno was the radio operator. David Cloud was the top turret gunner. Mack Harrelson was the ball turret gunner. Bill Zelensky was the bombardier. The crew was composed of Catholics, Jewish, and Protestants. The crew became very close as they trained together and flew 17 regular missions together. They played a lot of football in between missions and would pray together before the missions.

Crew of the *Pretty Gertie*. *Left to Right: back row- Cloud, Harrelson, Kiser, Johnson, Daily; front row- DeTunno, Zelensky, Kipper, Miller, and Crow.*

The *Pretty Gertie* was assigned to the 15th Air Force in Italy, the 772nd Bomb Squadron. Their primary objectives were to knock out the oil refineries in Polestia, Romania, to destroy the ammunition factories in Germany, and to target the factories in which the famous Panzer Tank was built.

Each plane would attempt 50 missions. The first 17 missions were mostly without incident, but on one mission as they were bombing in Czechoslovakia they had missed the target. They were adjusting the bombs and Colonel Kirks, a Commander of the 15th Air Force, found out that his lead bombardier didn't drop on the target, and so he ordered the whole 463rd Bomb group to make a 360-degree turn and go right back over the target. They all got very upset and started yelling at the pilot that they would bail out before they would go back. They had just seen planes going down on all sides. It would have been crazy to go back through because they had already dropped their bombs. Someone in the bomb group got on the intercom system, on the VHF (Very High Frequency), and began to curse Colonel Kirks. When everyone had returned to base, he tried to find out for days who had cursed him. He never did find out.

On October 12, 1944, H.C. left on his eighteenth mission. The crew was flying a brand new plane, a big plane equipped with radar in the ball turret. This plane had not been assigned to any crew. Members of the original crew split; some were flying on this mission, and some were not. The pilot was Lt. William Winters. He was a seasoned pilot who was ready to go home after this mission. They were just trying this plane out, so it was new for everyone. Lt. Irvin Kipper was the co-pilot on this mission. H.C. and Sgt. Doug Johnson were still the left and right waist gunners. Sgt. Fedoro DeTunno was still the radio operator and Sgt. Phillip Daily was the tail gunner. Sgt. David Cloud was the top turret gunner. The new navigator for this mission was Lt.

NOOSE DRAWS TIGHTER AROUND REICH

News clipping from *Stars and Stripes*, Italy Edition, Wednesday, October 4, 1944. Sent to Mr. Kiser from H.C. only days before being shot down. Reprinted by permission of *Stars and Stripes*.

Warren McCoy. Lt. Louis Martinich was the bombardier, and Lt. Thomas Madden was aboard as an observer.

They were shot down on this mission — the eighteenth mission. The evening before he was shot down, H.C. had read the scripture in 1 Peter 4:12,13, KJV, which says,

"Beloved, think it not strange concerning the fiery trial which is to try you, as though some strange thing happened unto you. But rejoice inasmuch as ye are partakers of Christ's sufferings; that when his glory shall be revealed, ye may be glad also with exceeding joy." On this mission, they were to bomb Rommel's army, which had retreated from North Africa and had gone back up into Italy into the city of Bologna. That morning as he prepared to go to the target, H.C. said, "I felt a gnawing inside that I would face a lot of trials because I remembered the night before reading in 1 Peter." They were to go over the target at 29,000 feet. This was the first time this crew had ever led the 463rd Air group. Perhaps there were as many as 1,000 to 1,200 bombers in the air that particular morning, plus the fighter escort that had escorted and protected them en route to and from the target. They were the first plane over the target, and the bombardier called H.C. over the intercom and said, "You see this dense forest; Rommel's army is camouflaged — bivouacked — in that forest; it looks as if it is going to be an easy mission." H.C. was a little relieved, but he still had a deep fear that this might be the time he would face "severe trials."

At 29,000 feet the first burst of anti-aircraft flak, the first burst of fire from the huge 88 mm. cannons down below, exploded directly under the B-17 bomber. The concussion from this exploding shell stopped the forward motion of the B-17 bomber. The concussion from the burst of flak sent the plane upward several hundred feet; then it started its downward plunge. Each of the crew members was pinned by centrifugal force as the plane went into a fast sharp dive. H.C.'s back was forced to the top of the plane, and he couldn't get back down to the escape hatch. The crew was praying for some way for the plane to level off so they could successfully bail out. The first prayer of the day was answered because with God's help, and the help of a good pilot, the plane did level off; and H.C. dropped from the top of the plane back down, hit on his hands and knees on the floor of the plane, and began to crawl back to the escape hatch.

At 29,000 feet, they were on oxygen, and it was 50 degrees below zero inside the fuselage of the plane. By this time, fire and smoke were coming out of the radio compartment. This huge bomber had four engines and one of the propellers seemed to be out of control, going faster and faster. H.C. could look out on either wing and see smoke and flames coming out of the engines. He knew, perhaps, it would just be a matter of time until the plane exploded. H.C. and Doug Johnson, both waist gunners, were to bail out of the same escape hatch. Their oxygen was gone, and they were gasping for breath. They knew that within a minute or so they would become unconscious without oxygen. H.C. prayed God would help them to make the right decision while they were still in their right minds.

H.C. had on fleece-lined gloves, and he crawled over to a metal door handle marked "Pull in case of emergency." He pulled his right glove off and grabbed the handle. His hand stuck to the door latch. Gasping for breath, he couldn't release his hand. The other waist gunner, Doug Johnson, came over and put his hand over H.C.'s. They both pulled, and the big door blew off into space. A 50-below-zero wind came rushing up and hit them in the face. They regained their senses from the blast of cold air and began to argue who would jump first — neither of them had ever jumped.

During the course of the argument, Doug pointed at H.C.'s chest parachute. His parachute had popped open when the plane was hit. The ripcord that he was to pull for a successful shoot opening was gone. The contents of the parachute had popped out into the plane and were scattered all up and down the waist of the plane. All of the springs that insure a successful opening of a parachute were bouncing around as the plane began to dive. Doug told H.C. he wouldn't jump because they were close friends. They had just played a game of football the evening before. Doug said he wouldn't jump without helping H.C., and there were no extra parachutes on the plane. H.C. told him not to risk his life. After much hesitation, Doug jumped. H.C. watched him as he cleared the plane and reached for the rip cord; he pulled it and the parachute successfully opened.

Right above H.C.'s machine gun was an oxygen bottle that he was to clip onto his parachute harness and plug into his face mask. The oxygen would last about eight to twelve minutes so that he wouldn't pass out while he was floating down into thin atmosphere. When the plane went into a dive, the bottle had come loose from its mooring. It was bouncing just like a football down through the waist compartment of the plane, but H.C. didn't have enough strength to chase it. He knew he was going to have to jump and probably pass out or maybe die from the lack of oxygen. He crawled on his hands and knees down through the fuselage of the plane, gathered up all of the tangled shroud lines and the canopy of the parachute, and crawled back to the escape hatch. H.C. had gathered the parachute into a large bundle. In fact, the bundle was larger than the opening out of which he was to bail. He kept trying to compress it small enough to get out of the door.

Finally he did this and began to pray: "Lord, I don't know what to do, but I just pray that you will help me make the right decision: should I bail out or should I ride this burning bomber down?" H.C. said, "I had seen many planes go down and they usually burst into flames. It seemed like the Lord just said, 'H.C., I am a God of miracles; and if you will just leap out into space with a torn parachute, I will show you that I am a God of miracles.'" Some time back in his Sunday School class, as a teenager, H.C. had a teacher who said when the book of Acts was finished that God no longer had to do these mighty miracles as He did when he was here among men. H.C. said, "I knew that if I was going to live, it would take a miracle from a mighty God."

He leaped out of the plane. As he saw the plane's rudder and tail section go by, he unfolded his arms and the parachute went up in a tangled mess. H.C. began to pray that God would open the parachute. He was falling faster and faster, and the parachute hadn't opened. H.C. began to make a lot of promises to the Lord. H.C. said, "I promised to witness every chance I got for the Lord Jesus. The parachute didn't open for a long time. I remembered back a few months prior that I had gone to the altar in my home church, Abingdon Baptist Church, and had given my heart to Jesus. I remembered how I accepted the blood that Jesus shed on Calvary's cross. I remembered that Jesus, who knew no sin, had become sin for me. I looked at my little Bulova wristwatch and I said, 'Lord, perhaps in the next few minutes I will face death because the parachute isn't opening, and I just want to praise you this morning for the fact that you have taken all fear out of death; I am not afraid to die. Lord, I am nineteen years old. If you would see to open this parachute, I will witness for you every opportunity. Lord, I am so young to die, and I am thousands of miles away from my Godly parents, grandparents, and my pastor. Lord, it is just you and I here now, and I pray to you. I haven't been a Christian long, Lord, but I pray you will let me live.' Still nothing happened. I told the Lord that maybe this problem was just too big for him, that even He couldn't open that tangled mess. When I told Him He couldn't, He showed me He could. The parachute opened with a terrific bang. I bit my tongue, my boots almost flew off, and I began to praise the Lord Jesus because this was truly a miracle."

H.C. says, "If we fail to recognize that God is a God of miracles, then we only have another religion — not a

25 October 1944

Mrs. Dacy C. Kiser
Route # 2
Abingdon, Virginia

My dear Mrs. Kiser:

I know that you must have been shocked by the report that
your son, Staff Sergeant Hiram C. Kiser, Junior, 33647511,
is missing in action and I hope that you will find the
following information encouraging.

On October 12, 1944, the Flying Fortress on which Hiram
was a gunner took part in a raid on enemy installations at
Bologna, Italy. Just as it reached the target the ship
was hit by flak and damaged so severely that it was necessary
for the crew to bail out. Since ten parachutes were seen
there is reason to hope that all of the men landed safely.
As soon as more definite news of your son is available it
will be passed on to you without delay by the War Department.

Hiram was well aware of the hazards involved in his job but
he loved his country and wished to serve her in the capacity
where he could do most to hasten the defeat of her enemies.
For his courage and devotion to duty he has been awarded the
Air Medal. His many friends here who feel his loss keenly
wish me to assure you of their sympathy and their hopes for
his safe return.

Very sincerely yours,

N. F. TWINING
Major General, USA
Commanding

Letter sent to H.C.'s mother from the Office of the Commanding General after H.C. was shot down.

personal relationship with Jesus Christ." And the Lord knows we have too many *religions*."

The plane H.C. was in was the first plane over the target. The parachute had opened successfully, and within seconds another group of bombers appeared. They were directly over H.C., and the target was directly under him; he was floating in between. He looked up and saw the bomb bay doors open, and these huge 500-pound bombs came falling, some in front, some behind, and some on either side. If one of the bombs hit the canopy of the parachute, H.C. would plunge to his death. He began to pray, "Lord, would you create a wind and just get me off of this target because one of these bombs will plunge me down to my death." No sooner had he prayed this than he began to rock back and forth like a pendulum on a grandfather clock. The wind was so great that at times it carried him above the parachute. H.C. says, "I knew that the God who made the universe had heard my prayers, that He had created this wind, and I just praised Him for it."

Soon he was away from the target area. He could see the famous 88 mm. German cannons firing in his direction. Floating downward, he was so close that he could see a streak of fire as the projectile left the barrel. He would time it, and sometimes it was six or seven seconds before the shell exploded. One time a huge shell exploded under him; his downward motion stopped, and he began to go back up. When the shell exploded under him, it almost burst his ear drums. H.C. was engulfed in the smoke and flame from the bursting shell, and he could hear thousands of pieces of jagged steel singing all around him. Yet there was not one hole made in the parachute. This was truly a miracle. H.C. said, "I know that an angel was protecting me and the parachute. I had another conversation with the Lord; I reminded Him that I was on my way down. I wasn't ready to go up yet; and sure enough, I

Dulag-Luft Germany

Date 20 Oct. 44

(No. of Camp only: as may be directed by the Commandant of the Camp.)

I have been taken prisoner of war in Germany. I am in good health — slightly wounded (cancel accordingly).

We will be transported from here to another Camp within the next few days. Please don't write until I give new address.

Kindest regards

Christian Name and Surname: HIRAM KISER

Rank: S/SGT. 33647511

Detachment: USAAF

(No further details. — Clear legible writing.)

Kriegsgefangenenpost

Postkarte

Mit Luftpost.

Par Avion

GEPRÜFT

Mrs. H.C. KISER

Empfangsort: ROUTE
town:

Land: ABINGDON
country

Landsteil USA
(Province, usw.)

Gebührenfrei

Postcard sent to H.C.'s mother from a transient interrogation camp, Dulag Luft in Wetzlar, Germany.

drifted over to one side, away from the combat area."

H.C. saw a building that he had thought was vacant and kept guiding his parachute toward that building. When he got 600 to 800 feet from the ground, he saw men running from the building. He realized from their uniforms that they were the enemy — the Germans. There were some huge hemlock trees that surrounded the old building. Two of the soldiers went back in the building; and when they returned, one had a machine gun and one had a rifle. They began to fire at him. H.C. says, "This was a terrible, helpless feeling, and I began to pray, 'Lord, please don't let me get this close to earth and be killed.'" H.C. collapsed the air in his parachute and got down between the men and the hemlock trees.

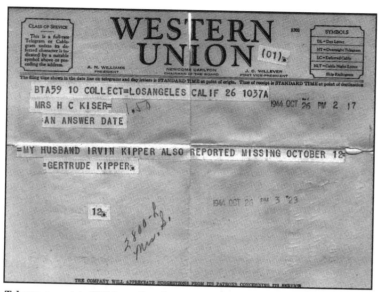

Telegram sent to H.C.'s mother by Gertrude Kipper on October 26, 1944, fourteen days after H.C. was shot down. Gertrude Kipper, wife of Irvin Kipper who was flying as co-pilot on the day H.C. was shot down.

My Dear Mrs. Kiser,   *November 27, 1944*

God has answered our prayers. I received a telegram from the government Friday night stating that my husband is a prisoner of war of the German government.

By coincidence, the same morning I received a letter from the bombardier on the crew, telling me that the latest rumor was that four of the boys were prisoners of war, four were safe, and two were still in hiding.

No doubt he knew the details but because I hadn't yet been officially notified he couldn't tell me for sure.

This should be considered good news and if you haven't heard anything official yet, I'm sure you will.

Please let me know when you do hear, as I am very anxious to hear of the safety of all the boys.

Very Sincerely,
Gertrude Kipper

Letter sent to H.C.'s mother by Gertrude Kipper.

Washington, GA
November 30, 1944

Dear Friends,

Your letter just received and we hasten to answer that you may know how we rejoice with you that your son is alive. Yes, it is hard to be glad that he is a prisoner but it gives a hope that he will come home someday.

We went to Atlanta to see one of the boys who had been in camp with our son, and we were relieved since talking with him. He says the boys are not badly treated. The German food is very little and hardly fit to eat but the Red Cross gives them a package each week (11 lbs.) And with the parcels from home they get along very well. The Red Cross had an abundance of food and clothing for this camp when he left the latter part of. July. He says the hardest part of being in the prison is the barbed wire fence and knowing there is no way to get out.

We have not heard from James in sometime - the last letter dated Nov. 11. So we are beginning to worry although we know the mail is not coming on time as it did when they first went over. We have not heard from Reid either. He has been a POW since Oct. 10, 1943. We have given our all so we can sympathize with you, but God is so near and has given us strength to carry on and He will be with our boys and girls where ever they are so we can trust Him for He is with them. We do admire your daughter she is so willing to do her part and we wish her the best of luck and God speed the return of our children. That will be such a happy day. We pray for your boy and want you to pray for ours too. We hope the little information we have given will be some help to you.

Excerpt of letter from Mr. and Mrs. J.J. Crow, parents of Jim Crow, the *Pretty Gertie* co-pilot, sent on December 4, 1944. Jim was not flying on the day H.C. was shot down. The Crow's other son, Reid, was also a POW, shot down and captured on October 10, 1943.

Chapter 5

CAPTURED

A thousand may fall at your side, And ten thousand at your right hand; But it shall not approach you.

(PSALM 91:7, NASB)

Just before H.C. hit the ground, he saw the two men that were shooting at him come running in the direction where he would land. H.C. asked the Lord for another miracle, "'Lord, as fast as I am falling, if You don't have a soft landing area, I will be crushed.' The Lord takes care of all details, so I landed in a swampy area up to my knees in something like muck or mud. I fell over backward and passed out."

When H.C. opened his eyes, two German soldiers were over him. One had knelt down and had a machine gun stuck in his left rib cage, and the other had a fixed bayonet mounted onto a rifle stuck in his right rib cage. They were looking at him and laughing. They were laughing: "This is an airman, this is a prize catch." H.C. closed his eyes as they were searching him and prayed, "Lord, if there was some way that I could speak German, I would love to share You with these German soldiers. Lord, it has been seven minutes from the time that I leaped from that burning bomber until my capture; and, Lord, I am not afraid of anything that might happen to me as a prisoner of war. I just want to praise You for saving me."

The two German soldiers took him into the old building. A German Luftwaffe fighter pilot was lying on a table. It looked as if one of his feet was just barely hanging on. A doctor was trying to help him. H.C. began to complain to the doctor about his knee. The doctor said he didn't have time to talk to him. Then H.C. saw Warren McCoy, the navigator, coming through the bushes toward the building. German soldiers were jabbing him in the back. McCoy's lip was busted. He had put his parachute on under his flak suit; and when he had pulled his ripcord, metal from his flak suit had slapped him in the mouth. The doctor asked them if they knew each other, and they both said, "No." They just smiled at each other; they couldn't reveal their acquaintance. The doctor prepared a pan of water and handed it and a piece of white cloth to H.C. and told him to take care of McCoy because he didn't have time for them. H.C. knew the lip needed stitches, but he did the best he could.

The German doctor told H.C. he would not let the mob of soldiers kill them, but that they needed to get rid of the airman's uniform. He saw H.C.'s name on his uniform and, recognizing the German origin of the name, asked, "You are a Kiser, why are you killing our people?" The doctor said that H.C. would find the cities of Germany flattened and that thousands of women and children had been killed as a result of American bombings. At the time, 20 or 25 German soldiers were wanting to kill H.C. They were chewing tobacco and drenching him with saliva.

The two German soldiers who had captured H.C. walked him out of the building and through an orchard. Green apples were falling everywhere as the earth shook from the firing of the huge 88 mm. cannons camouflaged in the orchard. The guns would go up toward the American planes flying up above, and H.C. would forget that the soldiers were gouging him in the back. They would try to give him a hand signal to get down. He saw them open their mouths, later realizing it was to avoid bursting their eardrums. There were four of the Germans, counting the two who had captured him; and when a plane came down, they would forget that he was there, and start congratulating each other. H.C., also forgetting his surroundings, would start screaming for the men in the plane to bail out.

Two planes were shot down as H.C. watched. He saw four men bail out of one, but none bailed out of the second; it crashed into the mountain and exploded. H.C. later read in a European newspaper about the planes that were shot down that day. The article reported that only one American plane came down that day—October 12, 1944—but he saw two shot down besides the plane he was on. H.C. said, "That was quite an experience standing there in that orchard; I now think of us standing there — the four Germans so happy that they were taking lives and me so devastated that my American partners were dying and going through the same fears and experiences that I only minutes before had gone through, only so many of them had not survived."

H.C. later talked to the pilot, Lt. Winters, about that day. H.C. told Winters that while he was being led away by the two Germans who captured him, he saw a plane with fire streaking out of it making huge circles and the wings were tilted inward. It looked out of control. When he asked him about it, Winters said, "Hiram, that was the plane you bailed out of." Winters explained he had feathered the engine or set the propeller to prevent the vibration. H.C. talked with another crew member, and he said the plane hit into the side of the mountain and exploded.

The German guards were leading H.C. down a path when a bomb came down and struck a big beech tree. A huge limb fell right in front of them. It made a tremendous noise. Though H.C. had been bombing for 18 missions, he had never witnessed first-hand the destruction and havoc, the American bombs had wrought. They had to crawl over the tree branches to continue. They hadn't gone 75 feet until another bomb went off. They saw a wagon loaded with bread being pulled by two horses. When the bomb went off, it turned the wagon over. H.C. and the guards had got there soon enough to see the bread still rolling down a steep grade. One of the horses was lying there dead, its intestines spread on the ground. The other horse was nickering, pawing at the ground.

There was a haystack out in the field. The guard carrying the machine gun was in front of H.C., and he said "Come on." They started to run; H.C. knew the guards were nervous. They wanted him to run with his hands up and when he put his hands down, the soldier would jab him with the bayonet and say, "Roust! Move! You are not going fast enough."

H.C. didn't understand why they were going out into an open field with a huge haystack. The haystack looked as if it had been there a long time. It had turned brown from the weather, and there was a pole sticking out of the top of it. The German soldier with the machine gun got in front of H.C. There was a hole about two feet by two feet, and he went down in that hole. By this time, H.C. was scared, and he just jumped through that hole. When he did, he saw that it was a concrete bunker. There was just a little light from a kerosene lamp hanging from the top. There were eight German soldiers on each side of the bunker. It was a reinforced concrete box. The Germans had a piece of plywood lying on their knees and they were playing poker. When H.C. dived in there, he hit the side of the plywood, and it and the cards and the chips went straight up into the air. The soldiers were cursing him. He was shaking and his teeth were rattling. H.C. tried to back up, but it was very crowded. There was one soldier who was his age, around 20. The young German would look at H.C. and smile. The other soldiers were much older. H.C. found a place to sit, and they put their plywood back up and dealt their cards just like there wasn't even a war going on.

When the planes had stopped bombing, the guards forced H.C. out of the haystack bunker. H.C. was relieved to see Doug Johnson also being held by German soldiers. The Germans put Doug and H.C. in the back of a jeep. A German sergeant was in the passenger seat and an enlisted man was driving. They were driving to the German headquarters, which were run down, but had once been a beautiful castle on top of a high ridge. The jeep was winding up the ridge and stopped at a house that had been bombed. It was a two-story brick house; half of the house was still standing, but the other half lay flat. It was about one o'clock in the day. One could see the upstairs. The Italian lady had made the beds, the covers were turned down, and everything was very neat. The family had a coal cook stove. A whistling tea kettle was sitting on the stove whistling. For a while they didn't see anyone, but suddenly they saw the Italian farmer who had probably been out in the fields and had come in for lunch. His family had all been killed. He had carried members of his family and put them in the back of a horse-drawn wagon. Two horses were hooked up to the wagon which was sitting on a slight grade. He had covered his family with a white sheet; and by the time the jeep H.C. was riding in had got there, the blood had soaked the sheet. The blood was trickling down to the ground from the back of the wagon. The Italian came running up to the jeep, his body gyrating. He was trying to cry, but he couldn't. They had stopped because part of the debris from the house had the road blocked. They had to move the brick out of the road so they could get through. The German soldier rolled his window down. The man was asking, "What can I do? Can you help me?" The German sergeant said, "These two in the back, they are responsible." The farmer was crying and went back to his yard and got an armful of bricks. He came back to the jeep and started to pellet the jeep with the bricks. H.C. and Doug were both large, and they were trying to get away from the window.

The jeep went further down the road, and there was an Italian boy, probably college age, well-dressed in dark pants and a white shirt lying dead beside the road; his hand clutched a black briefcase. He was lying face down; his body was torn. The jeep stopped, and the sergeant asked the driver to get the boy's leg which was lying about twelve feet away. The driver reached down, picked up the leg, and laid it down with the rest of the boy's body. The sergeant looked back at H.C. and Doug

Johnson and said, "You Americans don't care whether you kill Germans or what. That was an Italian college student."

The odor from Bologna was terrible. The 463rd was supposed to bomb the clump of trees, but some of the bombs went astray. The whole main street of Bologna was destroyed; power lines were down everywhere. H.C. could hear the sound of thunder as wires came in contact with each other. He could see blue flames like lightning. There was an occasional silence broken by the wail of sirens or the loud roar of bombs going off. The planes were equipped with self-timed bombs that would go off intermittently. If a building was hit and collapsed, the Germans were afraid to go in to rescue anyone because they didn't know when the next bomb would go off. Sometimes the bombs would go off at intervals of up to six or seven hours.

At the German headquarters, the captain took H.C. and Doug outside, and they could see the city. They were looking at a building, and he said, "I hope they don't hit that building there; it is for crippled Italian children." It plainly had a big red cross marking on it. It was a big building, almost as big as a tobacco warehouse. While they were standing there, a delayed action bomb exploded. The Germans would mark the ammunition buildings with a red cross. When the bomb had gone off, Doug Johnson, confronted the captain with the German's trickery and said, "Well, captain, looks to me like that was an ammunition dump or something."

The captain interviewed H.C. and all H.C. gave him was his name, rank and serial number. The captain looked at H.C., who was scared and pale, and said, "For you, this day, the war is over." H.C. was taken upstairs.

Johnson didn't have any respect at all for this German captain and didn't show him any military courtesy. H.C. was anxiously listening to Doug's interview. The captain asked Johnson if the American army had any discipline or courtesy for superior officers. Johnson replied, "Oh, yes, we will salute a general occasionally, but a little old captain like you, we wouldn't salute you." The captain cursed and said, "You stand up and salute me." Johnson got up and threw his hand up, then sat back down. The captain was furious. He said, "Johnson, you do it this way." Wearing spit-polished shoes, he clicked his heels together and said, "Heil, Hitler! You salute me; I am your superior. I want you to treat me with courtesy." Johnson got up and started clicking his heels together and sticking his hand out.

Then Johnson sat down on the table and said, "Hey Doc, how about a cigarette?" H.C. thought the captain was going to kill Johnson right there, but he handed Johnson a cigarette. Johnson lit up, took two or three puffs, and said, "That is the worst cigarette I have ever tasted." The captain replied that because Germany was at war with Turkey, they could not get domestic blends which were the good flavors. The captain added, "Your cigarettes are better than mine, I suppose, I haven't smoked one." Johnson said, "I have three or four left, and I'm going to give you one." Johnson handed him a cigarette, and he smoked it and said, "That is a good cigarette."

The German captain began to question Johnson about what type of plane he was in. Johnson, being sarcastic with the captain, said, "Well, captain, I'll be honest with you. It was a brand new plane, a huge plane. It had just come over from the states. I don't think even the pilot knew much about it. All he could do was take off and land it. It had so much equipment, we didn't know what all of it was." The captain had become very interested and wanted to know more. He asked Johnson to tell him what kind of plane it was. The captain would name every plane he knew the Americans had. He was well informed. Every plane the captain would name, Johnson would say "No, guess again." Then Johnson said, "Well, captain, if you really have to know, we were flying in a Piper Cub." Johnson told him that the Piper Cub had nine engines.

The captain became furious and said, "We are far superior to the American planes, and we have never had a plane with nine engines." H.C. couldn't believe it, but the captain actually laughed at Johnson. H.C. says that Doug probably saved their lives by his lack of fear.

Doug came upstairs where H.C. had been listening. A German soldier was lying in a bed with bandages around a stub where his leg had been. The captain made him get up and told him to guard H.C. and Doug. They had to sleep in the nasty bed. The guards brought steaks and potatoes up to H.C. and Doug. Johnson even made fun of that. He yelled down and told the captain that the steaks were tough; then he made fun of the coffee. The captain said that they weren't on good terms with Brazil. H.C. said, "Johnson if you don't shut up, you are going to get us both killed." Doug said that they were going to kill them in the morning anyway and he might as well have some fun. H.C. said the Germans must have thought Johnson was crazy because they let them live.

While H.C. and Doug were being held at the headquarters, they also heard the German captain interviewing Lt. Kipper, the co-pilot. He refused to give him any information other than his name, rank, and serial number. H.C. was afraid he would be killed because he was Jewish, but the regular German army respected the ability of these military officers. H.C. heard the German captain say, "Well, Kipper, would you like to know if Sgt. Doug Johnson and Sgt. Hiram Kiser are dead or alive?" Kipper started crying and asked, "How are my boys?" H.C. was greatly touched by Kipper's concern.

The Germans put H.C. in a local jail until they had a truckload of Americans. Then they loaded them into the back of a German truck, and they traveled through northern Italy en route to Frankfurt, Germany. The truck traveled during the night to avoid strafing and bombing by the American Fighter planes. A German sergeant was sitting over in the passenger seat, and he had a girl in the middle with an enlisted man driving. He would knock on the window and grab this girl and kiss her and say, "Look what I've got." She was as ugly as could be. The truck would look for Italian farmhouses at daylight to hide out. The guards would make the prisoners cut branches of pine or apple trees to camouflage the truck. The sergeant would knock twice; and if the Italians didn't open up, he would take his rifle butt and kick the door open and go on in. He would say, "Open up in the name of the Fuhrer." They scared the poor Italians to death.

The truck had pulled up at the home of an elderly Italian couple. There was a water pump in the middle of the farm yard, and H.C. saw the old Italian man pumping water for the livestock. H.C. took his tin cup over to get a drink. One of the Germans screamed at H.C. and threw a shell up into his gun. He was mad. He said that surface water gets into the pump, and he wasn't taking a bunch of prisoners with diarrhea. He made the farmer boil goat's milk over a big fireplace they had, and the Americans drank the goat's milk. The Germans found a wine cellar and brought out big bottles of wine. H.C. and the other prisoners were very thirsty, and they drank big tumblers full of wine. When they got back on the truck that night, H.C. said he didn't know where he was; it was the first time he had ever been intoxicated.

As they rode through the Italian towns, the GI's would yell at the Italian girls in English and the German guards would yell in German. In Verona, H.C. saw huge light posts; and as they got closer, he thought that the statues looked almost human. As they got even closer, he realized that they were humans. The Germans had hung dead men dressed only in their shorts on these light posts. It had rained, and blood was running down their bodies. They had big holes in their bodies where they had been shot. The truck drove through the town, and they had to circle back by these posts where six or seven bodies were hanging. Then came the realization of the terrible death and destruction they were part of.

Crew of the B-17 Flying Fortress shot down on October 12, 1944:

Pilot - Lt. William Winters - Escaped with help of Italian farmer
Co-pilot - Lt. Irvin Kipper - POW
Right Waist Gunner - Sgt. Doug Johnson - POW
Left Waist Gunner - Sgt. Hiram Clay Kiser, Jr. - POW
Radio Operator - Sgt. Fedoro DeTunno - POW
Tail Gunner - Sgt. Phillip Daily - POW
Top Turret Gunner - Sgt. David Cloud - Wounded - POW hospital
Navigator - Lt. Warren McCoy - POW
Bombardier - Lt. Louis Martinich - POW
Observer - Lt. Thomas Madden - POW

Chapter 6

INTERROGATION

*Let your conversation be
without covetousness; and be
content with such things as ye
have; for he hath said, I will never
leave thee, nor forsake thee.*

(HEBREWS 13:5, KJV)

H.C. and the other American airmen were put on a train in Verona destined for Wetzlar, Germany. In Frankfurt, they were transported by city bus. H.C. found that American bombs had also splattered that city. They were on these buses with civilians. When the civilians realized that they were prisoners, they would spit on them and would make them stand up in the front.

The truck load of Americans were taken to Dulag Luft, in Wetzlar, Germany, where they were interrogated individually. H.C. had a questionnaire to fill out; and he knew that if he filled it out to their liking, it would divulge many secrets about American bomb squadrons and bomb patterns. So he gave only his name, rank, and serial number as he had been trained to do. The German captain who was interrogating him read it. He could speak perfect English. He looked at H.C. and said, "Look at you: you have blond hair, blue eyes, your name is Kiser, but you spell it wrong. You are German, how can you do this — kill our people." He began to curse H.C. and said, "Kiser, I will classify you as a spy because you won't give me any information. Perhaps you bailed out behind our lines to destroy factories and railroad bridges. I will have you killed by either hanging or by firing squad." He said, "I alone make that decision. Do you understand?" At this point, H.C. was terrified and simply replied, "Yes, sir."

The captain ordered two guards to grab H.C. and drag him down a long corridor. The door opened to a concentration cell. Just as H.C. turned to go in, a German guard hit him in the back with a stiff rifle-butt plate. H.C. went plunging across the cell and hit the wall on the other side. The guard slammed the door, and it was total darkness. The stench was terrible. There were no toilet facilities. H.C. began to have a little pity party: "Lord, why did this happen? I am here waiting to be executed either by hanging or firing squad." The walls of the concentration cell he was in were about three feet thick. There was a pipe that came through to give him air from the outside. The pipe was about three inches in diameter.

In mid-afternoon when the sun's rays reflected through the pipe over onto the adjacent wall, H.C. could see a verse scratched on the wall by some previous prisoner: "I will never leave you or forsake you" (Hebrews 13:5). The Lord spoke to H.C. through that verse. H.C. read the verse and believed the promise. He challenged the Lord Jesus. H.C. began to pray, reminding the Lord that He promised never to leave nor forsake him. H.C. said, "I asked the Lord what I should do now that I was waiting execution. It seemed as if the Lord said, 'I am God, greater than any problem that you will encounter while a POW, and I am going to try your faith.' The Lord said for me to begin to sing a doxology, 'Praise God from whom all blessings flow, praise Him all creatures here below, praise Father, Son and Holy Ghost.' I will always thank God for appearing to me and allowing me to experience His awesome power. I found that God is a very present help in times of trouble and that He could change a filthy dungeon into a sanctuary." Just as Paul and Silas began to sing praises to the Lord and the walls of their prison cell came crashing down, H.C. realized that God is always present, and the walls of fear and anger came crashing down (Acts 16).

H.C. was in the solitary confinement cell for several days. He had been in darkness for so long that he could barely see when the guards came to take him to the captain again. He was taken back in front of the same German captain, who said, "That was a terrible mess you were in, wasn't it?" Again all H.C. could reply was, "Yes, sir." The captain gave H.C. the questionnaire and said he wanted him to continue filling it out. There was a question on it that asked his occupation before entering the U.S. army. H.C. wrote down that he was an American farmer. He then told the captain, "Sir, I have given you more information." The captain seemed pleased with himself and said, "Thank you, that is good, thank you very much."

When he read it, he became very irritated, his face became red, and he ordered H.C. to stand. A little table separated them. He pulled his steel helmet off and threw it onto the marble top of the table, where it was spinning like a top. He pulled his pistol out of his holster and stuck it against H.C.'s stomach. He said, "You know that I have the power to execute you, either by hanging or firing squad. Do you understand that?" Then he began to curse H.C., some in German and some in English. H.C. said, "I just bowed my head and prayed, 'Lord, I read that verse that you will never leave me or forsake me, and, Lord, you promised that I would get out of this camp alive. Lord, your word is at stake, and I don't know what you are going to do; but I pray that somehow or other you will take over here and prevent my being executed.'" H.C. was praying and the German captain was cursing. Then H.C. quit praying and the captain quit cursing. The captain looked at H.C. and smiled, put his pistol back in the holster, put his steel helmet back on. He reached out to shake H.C.'s hand. H.C. said, "I will never forget that handshake." The German captain said, "Kiser, normally I would have you killed, but I don't know what has come over me. I am going to let you sweat the war out in a prison camp." H.C. said, "Thank you, sir." God was at work all along, H.C. added.

Chapter 7

STALAG LUFT IV

*The Lord is my light and my
salvation; Whom shall I fear? The
Lord is the defense of my life;
Whom shall I dread? When
evildoers came upon me to devour
my flesh, My adversaries and my
enemies, they stumbled and fell.
Though a host encamp against
me, My heart will not fear; Though
war arise against me, In spite of
this I shall be confident.*

(PSALM 27:1-3, NASB)

H.C. was put on a train to go to Stalag Luft IV, Grosstychow, Poland, a permanent concentration camp for airmen. The train stopped in the city of Berlin, where the British Royal Air Force was bombing the railroad yards all night long. The German guards went to air raid shelters and left the American prisoners like sitting ducks to be bombed all night by the British. The Lord protected them, and they sustained the all-night bombing attack. There were a lot of holes in the boxcar; but as far as H.C. knew, no one was injured.

As the winter came along, malnutrition began to set in. There was a compound that held Russian soldiers adjacent to the compound for the Americans. H.C. described the desolation in the faces of the Russian soldiers as they stared into the camp. Many Russian soldiers starved to death or froze to death that winter — the winter of 1944. People were dying so fast in that compound that the daily bread ration was determined by how many could stand for roll call. Two Russians would take the corpse of one of their comrades and hold him up; it would be frozen stiff. The guards would come by and call them off; the two Russians would get the dead man's bread ration. Then they would drag him back and either stand him up or lay him down. They made use of corpses several times to get their bread rations.

The Germans stacked the dead Russians crossways, maybe eight high. They would wait until they had a load to bury them. The Germans would then load the corpses up in wagons pulled by horses, and parade them in front of the American compound. They stopped where H.C. and the other American prisoners could look at them before they took them to a ditch to dump them. They would laugh and say this could be the Americans.

If it had not been for the Red Cross parcels that

came to the American soldiers, the German threat could have been real. Thank God the Red Cross aid did help to sustain them. H.C. only received one complete parcel during the entire seven months that he was a prisoner. The German guards would steal them and use them for themselves. Whenever the American prisoners would get anything, the German guards opened every can or package, and it would spoil if it wasn't all eaten. They could never save anything for the next meal or the next day. They did this to stop the American prisoners from saving up food to use if they tried to escape.

The guard counted the prisioners several times a day. Each prisoner had been issued a spoon and a bowl. They were very important because the guards wouldn't give them their food ration without the bowl. The spoon, in later months, became a very important and useful tool for H.C. For roll call the prisoners would stand at attention and hold their bowl out in front of them. The German guards would come by and count them off. If the day was real cold and the Americans wanted to go back inside, they would stand still and stay in position while the guards counted. If the weather was good, they wouldn't want to go back in so they would let the guards count them and then two or three would run around to the next line to confuse the count for the guards. It was amusing to the Americans, sometimes keeping the guards out for hours. Some of the guards were on crutches and they could hardly walk. They had been wounded in combat and were assigned as guards. The Americans took advantage of that. The guards would count the prisoners several times a day if they got word that there was an escapee or other problem.

H.C. said that some accounts like <u>Hogan's Heroes</u> of digging tunnels, etc., were not true. The compounds were up on stilts. At night you could hear the collars from the German police dogs scrape across the bottom of the floor. H.C. said that was an eerie sound to listen to all night as

THE STARS AND STRIPES
MEDITERRANEAN

Vol. 1, No. 255, Tuesday, September 5, 1941 — ITALY EDITION — TWO LIRE

Allied Armor Frees Brussels; Yanks, French Occupy Lyons

Belfort Pass To Germany Goal Of Foe

ADVANCED ALLIED FORCE HEADQUARTERS, Sept. 4 — American and French troops today won occupying Lyons, France's second most important com...

Troops, Miles Apart, Win Town Of Pieve

ADVANCED ALLIED FORCE HEADQUARTERS, Sept. 4 ...

5th, 8th Advances Called Sensational

ADVANCED ALLIED FORCE HEADQUARTERS...

TROUBLE FOR JAPS

Nancy, Metz Said Taken By 3rd Units

STOCKHOLM...

BULLETIN

LONDON, Sept. 4 — Allied armored columns racing northward from the French border have liberated the Belgian capital of Brussels and, according to one correspondent's report, were within 25 miles of the Dutch border at noon today...

News clippings from *Stars and Stripes,* Italy Edition, September 5, 1944. Reprinted by permission of the Stars and Stripes.

15th AAF Heavies Blast Northern Italy

MAAF, Sept. 4—Medium forces, fighter escorted, of the 15th AAF heavy bombers continued their attack today against enemy lines of communications, striking at rail yards and rail bridges, supplying enemy troops in north Italy. One formation of bombers bombed submarines tied up in Genoa harbor.

Liberators with Lightning and Mustang escort attacked several bridges on the Brenner line between Bolzano and Verona. Other Liberators bombed rail yards of the same line. Early reports indicated no enemy airplanes were encountered. Slight to moderate flak was encountered.

Another formation of Liberators bombed Lake Latisana and Casarsa rail bridges, on lines leading into northeastern Italy. The Lake Casarsa bridge, last attacked July 5, is on the Udine-Trevisio rail line. Good results were reported at both bridges and neither flak nor enemy fighters was encountered.

Fortresses bombing submarines at Genoa met moderate to intense flak. It is believed the target was well covered by bombs.

Allied Airmen Composed Own Song Of Prison Camp

(By A Staff Correspondent)

BUCHAREST, Sept. 3 — Like "Mademoiselle from Armentieres," or any other soldier song, the words of "Bucharest Cannonball," the official song of the Allied airmen's prisoner of war camp here, cannot be traced to any one man.

You can't find agreement even on who started the thing, which, like Topsy, just grew into a multi-versed, almost endless, thing. And for some of the verses you'll have to get personal audience with any of the 1,000-odd men who remembers them—they can't go into a family newspaper.

The tune was a straight steal from "The Wabash Cannonball," but from there on all similarity ends. To give you an idea:

Across the Adriatic, through spacious skies of blue,
There came a thousand bombers, with airmen tried and true,
They headed through the Balkans and straight for Bucharest,
But when they reached Flak Alley, the gunners did the rest.

They all landed safely, with parachutes galore,
And now we're in a prison camp, a-sweating out the war.

A train pulled into Bucharest one warm and sunny day,
As we went through the city, we heard the people say,
"You're murderers, you're gangsters, you've bombed our city fair,
You've just knocked out our marshalling yards,
Which are now beyond repair."
But, we all landed safely, with parachutes galore,
And now we're in a prison camp, a-sweating out the war.

You may think that ends our story, with nothing else a-do,
We thought the war was over, but bombers they still flew,
We heard the roar of engines as they passed overhead,
We heard the bombs a-whistling and dived beneath our bed,
We lay there a-tremblin' and praying very hard,
That they would miss the city and hit the marshalling yard.

he lay there freezing, starving, lonely, and bored.

H.C. said that the only shower he got in his seven months as a prisoner was at Stalag Luft IV. They were put into a shower and for the first time they looked at their naked bodies and at each other. Their pelvic bones were protruding, their knees had swollen, their feet were swollen, their eyes had sunk back into their heads. They began to cry because they saw that their bodies were deteriorating. They would pray, "Lord, how long before we would get enough food to enable us to live." They would sit in the compound and have contests to see whose stomach would growl the loudest. They would try to laugh it off, but it was very hard. The prisoners would see the German guards smoking Camel cigarettes and know they were stealing the food parcels.

The food was so contaminated that they would turn off the lights before they ate it so they couldn't see what they were eating. Bugs would come to the top. Sometimes they would get just old cabbage leaves in water, not even warm. H.C. was eating the green soup one day when something squished in his mouth. He spit it out, and it was a little red mouse which he had chewed down on. He held it up and said, "Look here fellas, I've got fresh meat." Another man who had been there longer than H.C. said, "What are you going to do with it, Kiser?" H.C. said, "I'll die before I eat that." He said "Drop it over here." H.C. dropped it over in the man's bowl; he ate it, and was glad to get it.

H.C. was in this camp from October to February. He had never spent Christmas away from home. It was the Christmas of 1944, and his spirits were very low. On Christmas Eve, the guards told them that they could stay outside a few hours longer. The prisoners were locked up at three o'clock every afternoon. At around 8:45 p.m. H.C. was wandering around in the prison yard. He was very homesick and depressed. The guards had told the prisoners that if more than three of them gathered, they would be shot. There was a warning wire about two feet high and a sign that said in German and English, "Forbidden, Do Not Touch This Line or You Will Be Shot." Beyond this was an entanglement fence. The guards watched the prisoners from the big watchtowers. H.C. was so homesick, he felt he could reach out and touch the wire and maybe end the nightmare. They threw the search light on him. A friend of his who was in the same barracks saw H.C. and yelled out at him, "Kiser, you are about to crack up."

After they were locked up, H.C.'s friend invited him to come to his room. He said there was going to be some excitement. Boredom and depression had set in for the American prisoners. Twelve men had gathered in John's room, and they listened as he explained that an American doctor who was also a POW had been told by some German authority that the Russians were getting close and that the compound could be evacuated at a moment's notice. By this time, they had all lost a lot of weight and were barely getting enough food to survive. John said that they were going to pray and ask God for a miracle. The prisoners needed typhoid vaccines because when they were evacuated they would be drinking from unsanitary water supplies. John explained that as run-down as their bodies were, if a typhoid epidemic hit, they would die like flies. The twelve starved prisoners knelt down on their knees in a little semicircle on this lonely Christmas Eve. John said, "If any of you doubt, the fact that God will send a miracle — the typhoid vaccine — don't pray because God responds to faith when we pray." H.C. hadn't been a Christian for very long and asked, "John, how in the world is God going to get a vaccine into this prison! It has to come from New York through Switzerland by the U.S. Army Medical Corps." John said, "Hiram, that's not our problem; that's God's problem." They started praying. H.C. didn't know how he was going to pray like that. John began to pray, and suddenly he stopped and said, "Everyone, get off your knees, I just heard from the Lord that the vaccine is en route."

Days later, the prisoners were ushered into a big room and H.C. saw the American doctor. He went up and started cutting the lids open on the huge cardboard boxes that were stacked up. The insignia on the boxes was "U.S. Army Medical Corps." There were 2,200 men in that compound, and there was enough typhoid vaccine for each man. H.C. was in Compound D, and years later in talking with men who were prisoners in the other compounds discovered none of the other three compounds received the typhoid vaccine. (H.C. wonders now why they didn't ask the Lord for vaccines for the whole prison camp; he believes He would have supplied it.) The doctor came to John, who was crying like a baby. The doctor asked him if he was afraid of needles. John said, "No, I just realize the source of this medicine: twelve prayed and 2,200 received the vaccine." It was so impossible to H.C. that this could be, yet the Lord provided. It was a great lesson for him and one he continues to learn and teach.

Each of the four compounds in Stalag Luft IV had approximately ten buildings to house the prisoners. The buildings were divided into approximately twenty-four rooms. Each room was built to sleep twelve men, but almost every room had double that number of prisoners. Many men had to sleep on the floor the entire time they were prisoners; H.C. was one of them. Sometime after Christmas, Andrew Donato was captured and put into the same room with H.C. Andrew was a great singer, and they would all beg and bribe him into singing for them. He was bunked in the floor beside H.C. H.C. would nudge him in the side with his elbow until he would sing for them. He would sing, "Long Ago and Far Away" and "By the Light of the Silvery Moon." They all lay mesmerized as he sang the songs they had danced to with their high school sweethearts. H.C. said that they could lie and listen to Donato sing and dream of home. He said it was a morale booster for them all.

During his time in Stalag Luft IV the only possessions H.C. had were his Bible, bowl, spoon, an agriculture book from Virginia Polytechnic Institute and State University that he had gotten from a Red Cross parcel, his flight coat, and a baseball glove for which he had traded two packs of Camels. When he was interrogated, he had been issued a pair of coveralls and a pair of GI boots. The Germans had taken his nice fleece-lined flight boots. These were the only clothes he had the entire time. The Germans would allow a few of the prisoners to gather for a chapel service when Padre Anthony Jackson visited. He was a British POW who had been captured in Czechoslovakia, where he was a missionary. He told the American prisoners that they wouldn't let him come often; but when he did, a large crowd always turned out. He had only single books of the Bible like the Gospel of St. John. The prisoners would tear out pages and pass them around to someone else and then get another page. The men met in a very small and cramped building inside compound D. The windows were broken out, allowing the bitter cold air in. The men would try to cram things in the windows to stay warm. It was very crowded; they would squat down shoulder to shoulder and put their Bibles on their laps with their hands under their legs. They would sit like that for an hour and a half. The Holy Spirit would move through them and their morale would rise as they listened to the missionary. H.C. kept his Bible with him for the duration of the war.

H.C. and some of the others in Compound D became friends with one of their guards, Captain Wolfe. He had been a race car driver in the Indianapolis Speedway in 1937 or 1938. His sister and brother-in-law were in Chicago, where they owned and operated a bakery. When the war started, Captain Wolfe had come to Germany to look after his parents, and he was forced to join the German army. He had made captain fast. He was good to the American prisoners. One night, about 9:30, he knocked on the door of the barracks and sharply asked, "Is there one in here named John Schawbaur?" John was in H.C.'s room, and he jumped up. It scared John because he didn't know what was about to happen. Captain Wolfe called him outside and said, "John, I've got a sister and brother-in-law who own and operate a bakery on Cicero Avenue in Chicago. I notice that you have that address. Could you know anything about them? We are to believe they are hungry and not doing well. We are told that sugar and gas have been rationed in the United States." John told him, "Captain Wolfe, I have been in that bakery, but I didn't know who owned it. I've seen your sister and brother-in-law; they are rosy-cheeked, well-fed, and they have a prosperous business." He said, "Thank you, John." After that, he became even more kind to the Americans.

Chapter 8

THE FORTY AND EIGHT

*...but he who stands firm to the
end will be saved.*

(MATTHEW 24:13, NIV)

The prisoners were evacuated from this camp and loaded onto another train. They traveled on this train for eight days en route to Stalag XIIID at Nuremberg. While they were changing trains at Munich, H.C. counted 16 railroad tracks side by side. They had been bombed so thoroughly that only one track was running. H.C. watched the large Russian women who were prisoners working to keep this one track open. They had on bibbed overalls, blue shirts, and red bandanas. They were carrying steel railroad ties and placing them. They were lifting huge concrete boulders and throwing them in sinkholes — huge craters that had been made when the bombs hit.

There were five American airmen and six German guards. They had put six guards with them to keep the German civilians from killing them. Munich was one of the most bombed cities in Germany. The German guards put the Americans in an air raid shelter for the night. It was a huge concrete structure under ground; consequently, there was almost complete darkness.

Sometime in the early morning, a young lady came up to H.C. and wanted to know the time; she pointed at her wrist. When she looked at him and realized he was an airman by his flight jacket, she screamed! One could hear it echo through the whole shelter. When she screamed, she started to motion for the other German civilians and a crowd gathered around H.C. and the other four Americans. The guards told H.C. and the others to follow them, and three went in front and three behind. They took them out to a platform hoping to get on a train. The civilians were jeering and had drenched them with saliva by this time.

The crowd was getting closer and closer. The guards told them that they were trying to protect them, but that the people wanted to kill them because of the destruction of their city. They told the Americans not to make any facial expressions or show any sympathy or animosity, to keep blank stares on their faces. The German people were screaming and calling them "Americani swine" and "terror flyers" and "terror bombers." H.C. says he could see why they would have this hatred for Americans, especially airmen, because their city was in complete ruins from the bombing. As H.C. watched, while they were being drenched with saliva, he counted 22 infantrymen walk through the civilians. They were marching two abreast with one German guard in front and one behind. The civilians backed up to let them through, and there was not one word of animosity.

The guards headed H.C. and the other four Americans toward a small concrete room, a boiler room. A guard opened the door and everyone but H.C. and another POW pushed in. These two were so scared and wanted to get in the door so fast that they both tried to go in at the same time. They got lodged in the doorway; then the other POW went in first. Meanwhile the civilians were screaming and pulling on H.C.'s jacket. They were ripping his clothes when he lunged in. They slammed the door and were only about three feet from a furnace. The furnace wasn't running, so it wasn't hot. The German guards, H.C., and the other four prisoners made a human barricade. They put their feet against the furnace and their arms against the door. The crowd outside was stronger, and they would heave against the door so hard that sometimes it would open far enough that the prisoners could look out. It looked as if there were about 150 people out there cursing them. Suddenly they were in a game of tug-of-war that lasted for close to an hour. H.C.'s heart was thumping and pounding as they tried desperately to hold the door closed. Many times the civilians would open it about a foot, and the German guards and five Americans would almost give; then they would push and slam it together.

H.C. and the other Americans were put back on the train. At one stop, they wanted to know in which direction they were headed. They had a bread knife and gouged holes in the side of the boxcar. There were 55 prisoners loaded onto this one boxcar, called a "forty and eight," which had been designed for 40 sheep and eight horses. It was very crowded and did not have any toilet facilities. There was a bucket in one corner, and they all used it to relieve themselves; it was very humiliating. When the train stopped, they would dump the bucket and fill it up with nasty water for all 55 men to drink. The holes also allowed a little air in. The prisoners were dehydrated and almost dying of thirst. Another reason they gouged holes in the boxcar was that when it rained, they could take paper and fold it like a little funnel. As the rain went down the side of the car, it trickled down through that funnel and could soothe parched and bleeding lips.

The train had come to a halt outside the city of Englestat, Germany. One of the German guards, Captain Wolfe, knocked on the side of the boxcar and said, "Gentlemen, I've got bad news. You fellows have gouged holes in this boxcar, and the German SS (Hitler's elite guard) have found it. They are going to execute you for doing this. All they know is that you are airmen. You are hated in Germany because of the havoc and destruction you have brought to the German people. There will be a delay; they are setting up machine guns now, and some of the SS have gone into Englestat to bring back people to view the execution. I am going to do everything I can to ward off the execution, but there is only one of me and several SS, and you know their reputation."

Several minutes passed and true to Captain Wolfe's word, the SS pulled the spikes and the big door slid open. On a little hillside, about 50 feet away, were three German SS troopers with machine guns mounted on tripods. They were zeroed right in on the 55 men. They wanted the prisoners to file out, and they were going to shoot them down with machine gun fire; then the train was to pull out and leave the corpses there. When the door was opened and they saw their situation, some started crying and some started cursing. H.C. says, "I had so much faith in Jesus and had seen so many miracles in the past short months, that I began to pray: 'Lord, I praise you for this occasion. I don't know how you will stop this execution; but, Lord, at least we have seen the light of day today. I just thank you, Lord, for whatever means You will use to prevent this execution, and I will just praise you for it.'"

A fierce argument arose between Captain Wolfe and the SS. The German SS did not shoot any of the prisoners, but they ordered them to one end of the boxcar. They stood in the center and would grab them, run with them, and sling them into a pile inside of the boxcar. A few minutes later they dismantled the machine guns, loaded the men back onto the boxcar, and closed the door. H.C. and the other 55 men who were crammed onto the "forty and eight" went on to their destination. God had performed so many miracles and had become so real to H.C., that he felt he would never doubt Him again.

Hosea DeLeon, a Mexican who operated the ball turret position on a B-17 because he was small in stature, worked his way through the crowded boxcar over to H.C. He was gripping a little cross hanging around his neck and he was really scared. H.C. had been telling him about Jesus and talking to him about giving his life to Jesus. He called H.C. "Preacher" and asked what they were going to do. H.C. told him they couldn't do anything, and Hosea began to curse the Germans. H.C. told Hosea to let him finish the sentence — God was going to stop the execution. Hosea asked, "Preacher, how do you know God is real?" H.C. said, "I told him that when they closed the doors and let the train move, we would know."

When they reached their destination, they had been in this cramped boxcar, 55 men, for eight straight days.

When the train stopped and the guards opened the door, H.C. fell out onto the ground. A Hitler youth about 14 years old began to kick him and yell at him to move. H.C. says he knew he was very near death. He was sick, weak, and dehydrated. It was very humiliating and degrading to have this youth kicking and beating him with the rifle butt, gouging his back with the bayonet, and ordering him around. H.C. had not had a bowel movement in many, many days. He went behind a building and found a stick; he sharpened it as best he could and stuck this inside his rectum, pulling out a handful of dry, powdered waste.

The train had stopped at Stalag XIIID in Nuremberg. The prisoners were only there approximately eight weeks. The camp was adjacent to a railroad yard; and, again, the British bombed. H.C. says he could hear the big bombs coming in over them. They were in a thin-walled building and heard a bomb coming straight for their barracks. The bomb hit, the windows shattered, and glass flew. H.C.'s bowl was sitting on a shelf above him. In the explosion it fell and hit him above his right eyebrow. He ran to an air raid shelter outside. Another POW jumped in behind him and landed on his back. His shoes went down H.C.'s bony spine gouging the flesh off as he went down.

After the raid was over, H.C. and the other Americans went back to their barracks and H.C. realized that he couldn't see out of his right eye because of flesh that was hanging from his brow. There was not a doctor in the entire camp. H.C. had to take his thumb and put the flesh back in place, praying that God would heal it. Today one can't even see a scar where it was. It was a long, miserable night. H.C. was trying to hold that piece of flesh in place and trying to go to sleep. Still chilled from running out in the cold during the air raid, as H.C. began to get warm, the lice would begin to crawl all over his body, and he would awaken. H.C.

prayed they would leave that camp soon. H.C. said that looking back over his life, that had to be the longest night he ever had.

H.C. begged for a bowl from the German guards because he did not get even his meager ration of green soup without it, but they would not give him one. He found an old rusty tin can out behind a building. There was no water to wash it, so he dug down through the nasty muck of mucous and other waste to find a sandy soil to scrub the tin can as best he could, and he used it as a bowl. However, he developed dysentery after this. He also begged for a string. His pants had gotten so loose that he was having to hold them up as he walked. He never did find anything to use for a belt.

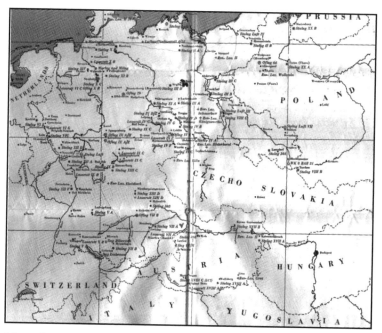

Map taken from *Prisoners of War Bulletin.* Published by the American National Red Cross for the Relatives of American Prisoners of War and Civilian Internees, February 1945. Courtesy of the American Red Cross. All Rights Reserved in all Countries.

Chapter 9

THE DEATH MARCH

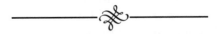

...and call upon me in the day of trouble; I will deliver you, and you will honor me.

(PSALM 50:15, NIV)

When the Russians got close, the Germans moved the Americans from Stalag XIIID, and they began the "Death March" or "Black March." The march was 80 to 100 miles from Nuremberg to Moosburg. There were about 15,000 American Air Corps, non-commissioned officers, and two American colonels in the group of marchers. There were several German soldiers as guards and one captain, Captain Wolfe. Some of the guards were walking, and some were on bicycles. The American prisoners marched in columns four or five miles long, and four persons deep. American planes, P-47 fighters and P-51 Mustangs, came over each day about noon. Not knowing that the huge army of men was POWs — thinking they were enemy troops, the Americans began to bomb and strafe their own with machine-gun fire. H.C. can still hear the screams. He would look back in the columns and see bodies of American soldiers flying through the air because their own planes were bombing and shooting at them.

The POWs knew they had to do something; they were desperate. They asked the German guards if they could gather anything white they had — clothing, anything — and spell out AAF (Army Air Force) and POW (Prisoner of War). H.C. had the book with him that he had gotten through the Red Cross, a book about agriculture from VPI. He also had his Bible, but said he would not tear the pages out of the Bible. They didn't use it, but they did use his agriculture book. It was a windy March, and they put rocks on the corners to hold the paper or material down. The letters were as tall as a refrigerator, and they covered a place as big as a room. The P-47s came over and banked up. H.C. saw one pilot look down and wave at them. They had been killing their own men, bombing in front and behind them. The next day they came over, but they didn't drop the bombs.

H.C.'s mother heard the famous news commentator, S. Gabriel Heater, report that a large column of prisoners had been spotted. They had been thought to be German soldiers and that our own fighter planes were bombing them and strafing them. Every day the news would report strings of prisoners miles long. Daily, the fighter planes would come over and get the directions of where the Americans were. His mother would listen to this every day, but she didn't know whether H.C. was one of the prisoners. While he was in Stalag Luft IV, H.C. had been given postcards that he could write seven lines on. He later found out that most of these were burned up. After the war, his mother received a few of them.

When the P-47s and P-51s were bombing them, the concussion from the bombs was terrible. The Germans told the American POWs that if they broke rank and ran, they would kill them. One guard came up to H.C., and H.C. told him that he was going to run. H.C. ran, and the guard grabbed him. H.C. said, "Don't be a fool; if we stay, the bombs and strafing will kill us." The guard threw a shell up into his gun and said, "No, no." H.C. started yelling, "Don't be a fool — they are going to kill us." H.C. fell down on his face; there was a tremendous roar, and fire was coming out of the machine guns from the planes above. He had the spoon that he used to eat when there was any food; now he used it as a shovel. He bent it to dig a hole to get his head into. The concussion would burst your ear drums. H.C. fell down, hit the ground, and looked over to his left. The same guard who said he would kill H.C. if he moved was down on the ground right beside him. H.C. tried to be friendly to him; and when the planes came over, the same guard would run to H.C. H.C. had him convinced that the fighter pilots had such sophisticated gear that they could read the German guards' name plates. The guard had been mean and had been cursing the prisoners. H.C. told him that he had better straighten up. The next morning, he had taken his name plate off. He actually

Supplementary Rations for Prisoners of War

By Clara C. Cerveny, American Red Cross Nutrition Service

The question most frequently asked by relatives of prisoners of war is, "Do American prisoners get enough to eat?" The first issue of PRISONERS OF WAR BULLETIN (June 1943) contained an article listing the contents of the standard food package made up and shipped by the American Red Cross. Since that article was published, the number of American prisoners in German hands has increased manyfold, and the same question is still uppermost in families' minds.

Relatives of prisoners are not alone in their concern. Several departments of the American Red Cross and various agencies of the United States government have been constantly concerned with improving the contents of the food packages and getting them regularly to the prisoners. One provision of the Geneva Convention Relative to the Treatment of Prisoners of War is that prisoners have the right to receive individual food packages. The International Committee of the Red Cross serves as the channel through which this supplementary food and other supplies are provided for prisoners of war. The American Red Cross prepares and ships all standard food packages sent from the United States to American and Allied prisoners of war, but is reimbursed for the cost of the packages by the governments to whose nationals they are delivered.

Contents of an American Red Cross standard food package.

Selection of Foods

The various items in the standard food package are planned, in the first instance, by the Red Cross Nutrition Service in consultation with the Office of the Medical Director. Each package, including wrappings and outside container, weighs 11 pounds. While the selection of items for the package is largely dependent on the availability of foods and of the packaging materials to keep them in first-class condition, the sort of food the prisoners liked and were used to eating at home is chosen insofar as this is possible. Each package must, however, provide the greatest possible amount of nourishment. The packages are planned to supplement the camp and hospital diets, which are likely to consist largely of starchy foods and to be deficient in proteins, fats, vitamins, and minerals. An attempt is made to supply, as nearly as possible, the minimum daily requirements of food essentials for an adult doing sedentary work.

Because the food packages may be in transit and storage and in widely varying temperatures for long periods before being distributed to the prisoners of war and civilian internees, the foods selected are so packaged as to be able to stand up well under such conditions for as long as 12 months. In view of the possible inadequacy of cooking facilities, only foods requiring little or no cooking are sent.

In order to prevent undue monotony, the items in the packages are varied as much as possible. Every package, however, contains certain basic foods, such as milk, oleomargarine or butter, cheese, meat, and fruit (dried). The other items vary, as do the kinds of meat and fruit.

The following are two typical standard food packages:

PACKAGE NO. A-1

Milk, whole, powdered	16 oz.
Cheese, processed American	8 oz.
Army spread (butter and cheese)	7½ oz.
Eggs, whole, spray dried	3 oz.
Beef, corned	12 oz.
Pork luncheon meat	12 oz.
Peanut butter	8 oz.
Salmon	8 oz.
Prunes or raisins	15 oz.
Jam	6 oz.
Biscuits, U. S. Army Type K5	7 oz.
Chocolate bar, Ration D	8 oz.
Sugar, lump	8 oz.
Coffee, soluble	2 oz.
Salt and pepper	1 oz.
Multivitamin tablets	16 tablets
Chicken noodle soup, dehydrated	2½ oz.

PACKAGE NO. 10-1

Milk, whole, powdered	16 oz.
Cheese, processed American	8 oz.
Oleomargarine, with added Vit. A	16 oz.
Beef, corned	12 oz.
Pork luncheon meat	12 oz.
Liver paste	6 oz.
Tuna or salmon	8 oz.
Prunes or raisins	15 oz.
Biscuits, U. S. Army Types 1 or 2	7 oz.
Chocolate bar, Ration D	8 oz.
Coffee, soluble	2 oz.
Salt and pepper	1 oz.
Jam	6 oz.
Multivitamin tablets	16 tablets
Sugar, lump	8 oz.

In addition to the foods listed, each package contains four or five packs of cigarettes and four ounces

Excerpts taken from *Prisoners of War Bulletin.* Published by the American National Red Cross for the Relatives of American Prisoners of War and Civilian Internees, April 1945. Courtesy of the American Red Cross. All Rights Reserved in all Countries.

Questions and Answers

Q. My son has been a prisoner of war in Germany since July 1944 and I have received only one letter from him. Can I cable him?

A. Cables from next of kin to prisoners of war may be sent only in cases of considerable urgency. If circumstances appear to warrant a cable, please consult the nearest chapter of the American Red Cross.

Q. My brother is in Stalag Luft I and we have been addressing mail to him, as directed by the Bulletin, to Stalag Luft III. As Luft III has been moved from Sagan, should we now send letters direct to Luft I?

A. No. All letters for American airmen should continue to be addressed to Stalag Luft III, with the subsidiary camp number (in your case, Stalag Luft I) added, until instructions to the contrary are issued by the War Department. Please see the item "Mail for Newly Captured Airmen" elsewhere on this page.

Q. When our prisoners in Germany are sick or wounded, will they inform their families?

A. If a prisoner of war is wounded when captured, the Detaining Power is required to report him as wounded, and, when this is done, the next of kin is so informed by the Office of the Provost Marshal General. German Lazaretts (military hospitals) are regularly visited by representatives of the Protecting Power (Switzerland), as well as by Delegates of the International Red Cross, and reports are made on the condition and treatment of wounded prisoners of war.

Wounded prisoners in Lazaretts are permitted to write home, and, if they are unable to do so, a comrade in the same hospital usually writes for them.

Q. Are our boys in German camps urged not to try to escape?

A. As a rule, the senior officer, or camp spokesman, does his best to discourage the men from futile attempts to escape. The test of a good spokesman is his ability to maintain discipline in the camp, and to keep cool in an emergency. It is a most important job in times of crisis.

Q. Is there any assurance that our fliers on bombing missions know where POW camps are so that they

A. The War Department knows the precise location of all officially reported POW camps, in the Far East as well as in Germany, and fliers are undoubtedly briefed to be careful to avoid bombing POW camps.

Q. Is it necessary for my husband, who is a prisoner of war in Japan, to file an income tax return?

A. While there is no exemption from payment of income taxes, legislation has been enacted which automatically postpones for prisoners of

(Continued on page 12)

PRISONERS RETURN

(Continued from page 3)

tion and already knew of the disability suffered. In other instances, however, the men were uncertain as to whether or not their families knew what had happened to them. It is probably fair to say of practically all prisoners of war that they worry more about their families than they do over their own plight.

The Voyage Home

There was marked improvement in the men between the time they crossed the Swiss border and the approach of their arrival in New York. During the voyage on the *Gripsholm* they had been able to be out on deck, and the weather was warm. They had enjoyed good food, rest, and relaxation, and the majority had gained weight. They were hungry for news from home and devoured the newspapers placed aboard the *Gripsholm* in New York and the copies of *Stars and Stripes* which were sent to the ship regularly while she was still in the harbor at Marseille.

The sense of humor of the returning prisoners was outstanding, and they always expressed a great interest when they learned that the person to whom they were talking knew something, even if it was only the location, of the camp in which they had been interned. Each person had a story to tell, and, given an opportunity, would talk readily about his personal experiences in camp.

Many of the men mentioned *The Red Cross News*, the monthly publication for American prisoners of war, which had reached some of the

Latest Information on Camp Movements

(By cable from Geneva)

Red Cross trucks operating out of Lubeck in the north and Moosburg in the south succeeded, during March, in getting substantial quantities of food packages to the prisoners of war evacuated from camps in the east who were still hiking across Germany. These marching columns were scattered over very wide area. In the middle of March, for example, an advance group from Stalag 344 was 30 miles east of Carlsbad while the rear of the column was in the vicinity of Bohmisch Leipa—the distance between these two points being nearly 60 miles. Likewise, the Stalag [illegible] near Melnik, to the Koniggratz region—a distance of about 75 miles. British prisoners constituted a large part of the southern columns, but they also contained Americans.

Similar situations existed in northern Germany, where about 100,000 American and Allied prisoners evacuated from camps in the second military district (particularly, in the case of Americans, from Stalags II B and II D and Stalag Luft IV) were walking across Germany to camps in the tenth military district. It was reported at the end of February that these men "were grouped in the vicinity of the Stettiner Haff, whence they will be conducted to Oflag X D (at Fischbeck), Oflag X C (at Lubeck), and Stalag X B (at Bremervorde)."

The Red Cross trucks delivering supplies to the marching columns had to search for the men not only on main highways but on secondary roads. The trucks operated under German escort, and, considering the chaotic transportation conditions which must now exist inside Germany, the authorities there have manifested a cooperative spirit in getting food, medicines, and other relief supplies to the men. It is an entirely new development in warfare to have Red Cross trucks, supplied and serviced by one belligerent, operating far and wide in the territory of an enemy belligerent.

Airmen from the Dulag Luft transit camp area are now being assigned to "the new Stalag Luft at Nurnberg-Langwasser," according to a cable received in the middle of March. This new Luft Stalag has not yet been designated by number.

Stalag Luft III at Sagan was evacuated on January 27. The men were given Red Cross food packages and were furnished some additional food by the Germans en route. The men were marched for three days on secondary roads to Spremberg—a distance of about 40 miles. They slept in barns along the roads. At Spremberg, the Americans from the south and center compounds were divided into groups of 2,000 and sent by train on February 1 to Moosburg (Stalag VII A), except for a few who were sent to Stalag III A at Luckenwalde. Americans from the west compound were dispatched by train from Spremberg to Nurnberg, and thence to Stalag XIII D, about eight miles from the city, which is probably "the new Stalag Luft" previously referred to. All letter mail from airmen, however, should continue to be addressed to Stalag Luft III until new directions are given.

A cable from Geneva on March 10 stated, "Oflag 64 proceeding by rail toward Hammelburg." An earlier message had reported that about 500 American (ground force) officers from Oflag 64, "travelling by rail, were near Parchim (southeast of Wismar on a line between Wismar and Berlin), awaiting transport for Hammelburg." Oflag XIII B and Stalag XIII C are the only prisoner of war camps known to be in the vicinity of Hammelburg. Several hundred American officers formerly at Oflag 64 were liberated by the advancing Russian armies and have returned to the United States.

thought H.C. and the other prisoners could be talking to the fighter pilots.

There was no food along the death march, only what they could steal or find on the road, and that wasn't much because it was March. There was nothing to steal out of the fields. Sometimes, if they were fortunate, they would stay at a barn and would steal potatoes or grain. They ate the grain and potatoes raw — anything to sustain life. H.C. would grab a handful of wheat, and there would be rat droppings mixed in it from the floor of the barn. He would pick them out, throw them down, and eat the wheat. One night, they stayed in a barn that belonged to an affluent German farmer. He had several Polish girls who were servants or slaves on the farm. A pretty, tall Polish girl, with long, black hair was cooking potatoes in a large cooking vat to feed the hogs and cattle. H.C. asked her for "kertofile," meaning potatoes. She said she would leave him some in the vat, but for him to wait until she went back into the house. There must have been a dozen large potatoes. H.C. lined the inside of his jacket with them. H.C. said that it was a beautiful feeling to know that he would have food for supper and food for another day. He slept like a baby that night, knowing he would have food tomorrow. He knew firsthand what it meant when we say, "Dear Lord, give us this day our daily bread." Soon after this, they quit letting the prisoners stay in barns. The Germans said the prisoners were so nasty; and they were urinating on the hay, and the cows wouldn't eat it!

One particular night of the march is still very vivid to H.C. The prisoners had bedded down in a huge forest. Still March, it began to rain. The rain turned to sleet, and the sleet turned to ice. H.C. was afraid he would freeze to death. He had an overcoat that he took from one of his friends who had died, and he used it for a blanket. The next morning when he woke up, the overcoat was frozen stiff with ice. The guards tried to wake the prisoners. Many of them had died. H.C. took the overcoat that was frozen into a sheet of ice and leaned it against a tree and started to walk. He had lost all feeling in his body; his feet were frostbitten. He looked back at all of the men just left lying there frozen stiff with a skift of snow over them. H.C. and some of the other prisoners begged to try and move the bodies to see if they were still alive, but the guards made them keep moving.

They started walking up a hill, and H.C. said, "Please, Lord, don't let me suffer this hell and then be killed." A friend, James Mosby, got behind H.C. and started to push him up the mountain. He grabbed H.C., shook him, and began to curse him. He said, "You are about to give up, and I thought you were tough; I thought you were a hunter." Of course, H.C. knew James was doing this so he would get his mind off his pitiful condition.

H.C. fell when James turned him loose, and a German guard came upon him. The guard reached into his overcoat and took out a piece of bread. He sliced it and held it out to H.C. H.C. was lying down, and as he reached for it, the guard would jerk it back. He would hold the bread out to H.C. time and again, and H.C. would reach for it; the guard would jerk it away. Then the guard would either eat it or give it to his dog, a big German police dog on a leash. H.C. was so hungry, so desperate. The guard reached into his other overcoat pocket and pulled out a block of cheese. He would offer it to H.C., then jerk it back. H.C. learned that no matter what the situation, if you are starving and someone hands you food, you will reach for it every time. By this time H.C. had gathered enough strength that he cursed the guard and lunged at him. H.C. was shouting in a raspy voice, parched from thirst and weak with hunger, that he hated him and that some day he would kill him.

His feet were completely frozen. He had no control of his bowels or bladder. He was running a high fever and when he had a bowel movement or his bladder emptied, it would just run down his legs and freeze. One night, he tried to take his boots off. His feet were so frozen and swollen that he could hardly get them back on. After that, he went for weeks without taking them off.

Several days later, they were marching through a small town in Germany. H.C. saw a plank fence and realized that there had been a garden there. He saw that some leaves of cabbage had been pulled, and a few leaves were lying on the ground. They were shriveled and bleached out, but to H.C. they looked delicious. H.C. had named the guard Jim who had tempted him with the bread and cheese. He said, "Jim, I'm going to get those cabbage leaves. I'm starving." The guard replied, "I'll shoot you if you do." H.C. was feeling delirious, and he was filled with hatred for Jim. He wanted to make Jim feel little because of what he had done. H.C. got on top of the fence, and just before he went over the fence to the other side, Jim hollered again, screaming, "Halt, don't go." This time he put a shell into his gun and took aim at H.C. H.C. said, "Jim, wait just a minute before you shoot me," and H.C. began talking to the other prisoners.

A big crowd had gathered, wanting to see a little excitement because normally they didn't argue with the guards. All of the other POWs were listening to the conversation. H.C. stretched his arms out in a helpless position and said, "Fellas, Jim is going to shoot me. He is going to shoot me for going over here and getting cabbage leaves." Then H.C. looked Jim in the eyes and cursed him, he called him several names and told him he didn't have the guts to shoot. H.C. went across the fence, got the cabbage leaves, and ate them. Jim's face was flushed; he hated H.C., and H.C. hated him even more. Several of H.C.'s buddies came up and said, "Kiser, we thought you were a Christian, we saw a side of you we didn't even think was there." H.C. began to curse them, his own friends — close friends — and told them he didn't want to hear that.

The march continued and H.C. talked to the Lord, "Lord, I'm not sorry that I cursed Jim and the others. I read in the Bible when the Israelites were coming out of Egypt and they were hungry, you rained bread and quail for them." He prayed, "Lord, I am your child, too. Right now I know perhaps you don't want to claim me, but whether you like it or not, I'm your child. I've been saved, born into your family and truly I'm disobedient. But Lord, I'm hungry, I'm starving." The Lord could have struck him dead right there, but instead of rebuking him, Jesus kept saying, "H.C., I love you, I love you. I'm preparing you for your life ahead. These trials will give you strength as you go through your life. This is all part of my plan for your life."

Chapter 10

STALAG VIIA
AND A LOAF OF BREAD

*I was young and now I am
old, yet I have never seen the
righteous forsaken or their
children begging bread.*

(PSALM 37:25, NIV)

The prisoners reached their destination, the final camp, Stalag VIIA, in Moosburg. H.C. was in this concentration camp for five or six weeks before liberation. By this time, he was in very bad shape. He was staying in tents with hundreds and hundreds of prisoners. They didn't have flashlights; they didn't have any provisions — no food, no blankets, nothing, just what they had carried into the camp with them. When they had to urinate or have a bowel movement, they would climb out and step on different people to try to get outside. H.C. had lost control of his bodily functions and never did get all the way outside. He would attempt to get back to his blankets. Very weak and near death, he would stumble and fall. Someone would shove him and curse him. Everyone was like that. He heard cursing all night; they were stepping on each other — desperate, a mass of starving, dying men. The odor was terrible; no one had underclothes. There were no clothes to change into. H.C. became so depressed; death might have been a relief, but the Lord kept saying, "H.C., I am preparing you for storms that will come later in life."

There was a doctor in the camp, a member of the Royal Air Force, a medic who had been shot down. H.C.'s friend, James Mosby, was stronger, and he convinced H.C. to go see him. H.C. couldn't walk; he had to scoot on the gravel trying to get to the doctor. As he approached the doctor, he found enough physical strength to stand up. The doctor smiled at H.C. and said, "Kiser, I've got good news and bad news. The bad news is that you are going to die, and the good news is that you will die quickly." He told H.C. that with the high fever, dysentery, and malnutrition he would die easy, perhaps that night, in his sleep. H.C. said, "Listen, doctor, I didn't want to come to you to start with, and I'm not going to die. But I am desperate: what can I do?" The doctor said, "You know, back in Ireland we raised sheep, and I have seen my father take one of the sheep that had diarrhea and take soot, chimney soot, mix it with water, and pour it down the lamb's throat; sometimes they would get better, and sometimes they would die." He said, "Why don't you get some soot and drink it, but the thing you really need is a loaf of white bread." H.C. scooted back to the tent. The only things he had then was a baseball glove, a Bible, a rusty tin can to eat out of, and a spoon. He went to an old chimney and got soot, mixed it with water in the can, and drank it.

Before H.C. went to bed that night, he prayed, "Lord, you are going to send me the bread before it is too late, and I want to give you thanks tonight for the bread because when I get it — me in this starved condition — I will eat it before I praise you and thank you for it." He thanked God for the bread, giving thanks because he would receive it simply by faith, not because he was demanding help from the Lord. H.C. knew the Lord would provide in his time of need, in His way and in His timing.

A day or two passed, and a friend of his — a former crew member who bailed out the same day he did, the top turret gunner, David Cloud — walked up behind H.C. and pulled H.C.'s jacket open and stuck a loaf of bread there. H.C. looked up and thanked Jesus first. H.C. asked David, "How did you know that I was starved and I needed a loaf of bread?" David said, "Hiram, I knew some airmen prisoners were coming to this camp, and I reckon the Lord told me that I would find you starved. I had access to a loaf of bread, and I took that bread and started to find you." He came straight to H.C., perhaps, 10,000 to 12,000 other prisoners of all nationalities were in the prison camp, and he came straight to H.C. with the loaf of bread. Praise God, what a miracle!

David Cloud was popular among the Germans. He had been wounded and was in a German hospital barracks. When they had nursed him back to health, David then waited on Germans who were wounded. They liked him because he had a good personality and had good rapport with the German authorities. He found H.C. a place to stay inside the hospital barracks. H.C. had a little food to eat then and a place to sleep. So after he had gained enough strength to walk again, David said, "Now, Kiser, I'm going to get you outside of this camp." H.C. didn't understand exactly what he meant. There was a Catholic church inside the little town of Moosburg, about a mile and a half away. Downstairs in the basement there were potatoes for the German population of the city of Moosburg. Upstairs in the church were Red Cross food parcels, when anyone was fortunate enough to get one. Every camp had an American liaison for the Red Cross, a man of confidence. He would talk to the Germans when a prisoner got out of line; he would be an advocate for the prisoners. David Cloud was this person in Stalag VIIA.

David said, "H.C., if you feel like going to town, I will go with you on the first trip. I will get you on the Red Cross food distribution list, and this way you will get outside the camp." So David and H.C. talked to the German guard, and David gave H.C. a number in German. H.C. said that when the big gates went open, he felt like a bird out of a cage as they walked down a beautiful path into Moosburg. When they got to the church, they were not supposed to talk to the Germans. They were just to walk around and around the church and if they saw anyone trying to break into the church, they were to tell the German guards. It was an agreement with the American Red Cross. The German guards were also walking around, and sometimes it would be completely dark. One of the Germans guarding the church wanted to get soap, cigarettes, and a little chocolate bar that came in the Red Cross food parcels. With the cigarettes and chocolate bars — a luxury — the guards could trade them for favors. H.C. would give the guard soap in exchange for bread or something. One night H.C. asked him what he was doing with all of that soap. He was very honest and told him that the last time he went home, he stank so badly that his wife wouldn't let him sleep with her.

David and H.C. knew the potatoes were in the basement. One night David got H.C. a parachute bag and said, "I am going to take this guard around here; and when you hear me cough a couple of times, you know that it is time for you to go through the basement window." In a little while, he coughed several times; and when he did, H.C. bolted through the little window. He landed on the potatoes and just started rolling down. It was pitch dark, and H.C. didn't think: he just started putting potatoes into the bag. He finally filled the bag and started up toward the window. He felt as if he was suddenly on a treadmill; he was going backward. He would climb up and fall backward. He grabbed the rafters and threw the potatoes up and lodged them. When he got up there, David was standing by the window. H.C. started hitting him in the leg. David was stomping, and whispered, "Don't come out here yet. I have to get the guard back there; he is standing right beside me." David walked back around the church and coughed a couple of times. H.C. threw the potatoes out, then he climbed out. They took the potatoes back to the camp, and a lot of starving men were glad to get them.

H.C. started going out on his own. The German guards would talk to him; but if their superior came up, then they would start cursing H.C. As soon as their superior left, they would apologize. H.C. says, "I didn't think anything about it. It was all part of the game of survival; we were all stuck there, and none of us wanted to be." H.C. certainly didn't want to be there, nor the other thousands of prisoners — not even the German soldiers.

En route to the church, there was a big white affluent home, and a very beautiful French girl lived there. She was a servant to the family. She would take pastry, bread, and eggs, and put them in tall grass for David and H.C. She fell in love with David Cloud. He hadn't been in a concentration camp, and, being in the German hospital, he hadn't lost any weight. He was a tall, good-looking man and a charmer. One day, when H.C. was out on his own, he went over to the grass where she would leave them food, and she had a letter there to Mr. Kiser. H.C. couldn't even talk to her since she spoke French. He went back and found Dave and said, "Dave, I took your girlfriend away, she wrote me a letter." Dave opened it, and he had somebody to interpret it for them. She said, "I like you, Mr. Kiser, but David is the one I am in love with."

One time H.C. went back to the camp and had forgotten the number they gave him; they locked him outside, and the guard wouldn't let him come in. They had seen him, but he had to give the number. H.C. asked them to get David, who identified him. All of that time, he could have just gone out in the fields and escaped, but he had given the Germans his word of honor. If anyone escaped the guard detail, they would cut food parcels for the other prisoners. H.C. couldn't escape; even though he had many opportunities, he wouldn't.

H.C.'s spoon, used more as a shovel; his ball glove used as a pillow, his Bible giving him spiritual food. These three items (pictured on the cover), along with his flight jacket used more as his blanket, were the only items H.C. had during his imprisonment. These items were so precious to H.C., he would not leave them behind.

Chapter 11

LIBERATION DAY

*Not only so, but we also
rejoice in our sufferings, because
we know that suffering produces
perseverance; perseverance,
character; and character, hope.
And hope does not disappoint
us, because God has poured
out his love into our hearts
by the Holy Spirit, whom
he has given us.*

(ROMANS 5:3-5, NIV)

On the day the Americans were liberated, April 29, 1945, H.C. and the others heard cannon fire. They could hear when the big tanks came out of the grass, and then went up on to the hardtop road. They could hear the clanging and the cleats. They could hear the loudspeakers, but they were too far away to understand; they could just hear the blaring. SS troops were in the steeple of the little white Catholic church. They took machine guns and were going to fire at the Americans coming in their tanks. The Americans said they did not want to destroy the church, but if the Germans did not surrender, they would blow the steeple off. The SS troops coming into the camp started ordering the Wehrmacht troops, the enlisted men of the German army, to set up machine guns and keep Patton's Third Army from coming in. The German guards that H.C. had known all this time got very nervous and said they were not going to defend the camp.

The SS and the Wehrmacht started shooting at each other. H.C. watched them carry in an SS trooper on a stretcher; he thought the trooper was dead. He was in a puddle of blood. They brought him in and laid him down. The Wehrmacht would go by and kick him. There was so much animosity between the Wehrmacht and the SS. H.C. couldn't believe that these people, both Germans, would hate each other. There was hatred everywhere. The Wehrmacht were constricted people just as the American prisoners were. They wanted the war to end and the SS wanted a big fanfare. They were shooting each other right and left. That puzzled H.C. How could they do it?

The Germans surrendered to Patton's Third Army. The 14th Army Division made the German soldiers march into a huge building, almost the size of a tobacco warehouse. They had to throw their guns and ammunition down. Then the American soldiers lined the German guards up around the perimeter of the wall. They set up a kangaroo court, and they let the prisoners be the judge. If a guard had been good to a prisoner, the prisoner could spare the guard's life, by simply saying so. But if any had harassed prisoners, deprived them of food, or maimed anyone in any way, he was pointed out and was killed. H.C. could hear sporadic gunfire, and several ruthless guards were being killed. They were being led at gunpoint over a ridge about 50 from the building they were in. Many of the troops that had come in to free the American prisoners were crying; they would look at the prisoners and cry at how pitiful they all looked. They were filled with rage at the way their American comrades had been treated. H.C. began to recall the time when he was captured and had a gun and bayonet stuck in his back. H.C. knew his life had been spared.

The American prisoners were lined up and were going around to each of their guards, making the decision whether to let them live or have them killed. It was a terrible decision to make. H.C. shook hands with some of the guards who had been kind to him, and he wished them Godspeed. He came to Jim, who had tempted H.C. with bread and cheese on the death march. Jim was still in good physical shape. They were both about 6'2"; they were literally face to face. H.C. had entered the army weighing 176 pounds and, now weighing about 86 pounds, stood before Jim. H.C. began to curse him and said, "Now, you are the POW, and I am the free man." Jim would never make eye contact with H.C. and became short of breath; at this moment he knew that H.C. could have him killed.

Perspiration began to come out of Jim's khaki uniform, and H.C. bowed his head and prayed, "Lord, help me to make a decision here. Should I have this man killed? You know what he did. What should I do?" Jesus said, "H.C., you know when you were dead and trespassing in sin, I shed my blood on Calvary's cross, and I forgave your sin. If you have this man put to death, then he will die and go to hell. Why don't you forgive him like I forgave you?" H.C. said, "Thank you, Jesus." He reached out and shook Jim's hand. H.C. says, "I will never forget that strong grip and the smile that came on his face. I just praised the Lord that I had the opportunity to forgive him like Jesus had forgiven me. There was something in that handshake; we couldn't speak each other's language, but I could feel and communicate Jesus' love and forgiveness. God gave me that grace. It was a great turning point in my life, an event that I will never forget; and I don't ever want to forget. I draw strength from this every day."

After Liberation Day, H.C. never saw David Cloud any more. Patton's troops told the prisoners they should stay in the camp or stay in a group. One of the Americans tossed H.C. a little box of Grapenuts, a small individual serving box. He opened it up and would pinch a little bite. It was the best stuff in the world. They warned the prisoners about eating all they wanted, that their stomachs had shrunk, and it could kill them.

H.C. walked out of the camp a couple of hours after liberation. He was a little afraid of going outside the prison, but he did go to one house outside the prison camp. It was a small German farmhouse with outbuildings and an orchard. The German farmer was glad to see him. He had a young granddaughter there. The Russians were rushing out of the camp, two of the Russians had a sow which belonged to these people. One had hold of her back legs, and the other was beating her with a club. She was squealing and blood was running out. "They killed that old hog and just ate the meat raw," H.C. said. "The Russians were screaming and running everywhere; it looked like a football team running out onto the field. The Russians were grabbing chickens. One man had a chicken under his arm, and he was plucking feathers off and throwing them around. He was gnawing down on the chicken; he didn't even wring its neck." The poor old German was scared to death. He told H.C., "If you'll stay here and guard my house — being an American, I'll let you sleep with my granddaughter." Everyone was that scared. H.C. didn't stay with the Germans — he couldn't comprehend how cruel everyone was. So much had happened to him in seven months. The experiences changed his life — they changed everyone's lives.

The regular co-pilot, Jim Crow, was not flying on the eighteenth mission. Jim said it was a sad day when the rest of the *Pretty Gertie* crew didn't come back in. He had to go into the tent and gather the crew's belongings to be mailed home. After his crew was shot down, Jim was made first pilot on a mission to Blechhammer, Germany. They were bombing the tank factory, and the plane he was flying collided with another plane in the clouds. It went into a spiral and was going down. He had given up to die when the plane exploded. He revived, pulled his rip cord, and about two seconds later hit the ground. Jim also became a POW. H.C. saw Jim at the prison camp, Stalag VIIA.

On Liberation Day, Jim said the prisoners wanted to get a firsthand view of Patton's army coming in and seeing the swastika come down and Old Glory go up. Nearby, there was a little building about eight feet tall and they climbed on top of it to get that view. Jim said that when the POWs would run and stick their hands up, he would pull them on. Jim said, "I saw this guy stick his big hands up, and it was a black man. He was a P-51 pilot, our escort. The old hatred began to melt and I realized that the man I was going to help up was better coordinated than I, even smarter than I. I thought, 'He will go back to Atlanta, and the best job he will be able to find might be owning a shoe shop or something.' When that American flag went up, the black man stood at rigid attention and tears were streaming down his face. That one thing changed my whole attitude toward blacks forever."

They were transported from Stalag VIIA by army trucks to the Landshut Germany Air Strip. They put the POWs on C-47 transport planes and flew them to a transient camp in the heart of France, in Le Havre, called Camp Lucky Strike. They deloused them and taught them to eat again. Many of the Russians just gorged food, and a lot of them died.

Nine of the ten members of the crew on the eighteenth mission were captured and in POW camps, all except the pilot. When the plane was shot down, Winters was wounded. It was a flak wound in his leg. Winters was lying on the ground where he had crawled into a fence row. He had pulled up grass and camouflaged himself. He was bleeding profusely. German soldiers were going by, but he wanted to surrender to a military officer. He said that he figured an officer might have more respect for him. An officer never came by. He took his T-shirt off, made a tourniquet, and got the blood stopped. He finally saw an officer go by within 20 feet. Winters said, "I tried to get his attention, and I did. He turned and looked at me lying there, and he gave me a Heil Hitler salute, clicked his heels together, and kept going. He wouldn't capture me."

Winters said he knew the Italians had a good underground system. A young Italian farmer found him lying there, picked him up, put him over his shoulder, and carried him to his house. He kept him there and doctored his wounds. After about a week, he put him in a hay wagon, lying flat with his face down toward the cracks in the bottom of the wagon. The farmer covered the wagon with hay. He had started down a road when German soldiers stopped the wagon and ordered him to give them the hay. Winters said the Italian farmer was very scared; his voice was trembling, and he said, "Please, this is all I have for the winter." A German guard got on top of the hay with a pitchfork and started pitching the hay off the wagon. Winters said, "I was lying there waiting to be stabbed in the back." The German stopped just before he stabbed

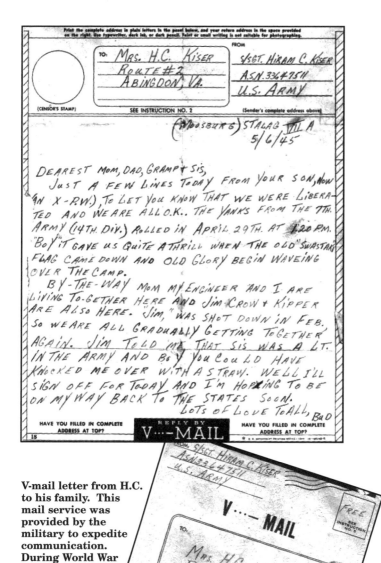

Print the complete address in plain letters in the panel below, and your return address in the space provided
on the right. Use the typewriter, dark ink, or dark pencil. Faint or small writing is not suitable for photographing.

TO: MRS. H.C. KISER
ROUTE #2
ABINGDON, VA.

FROM
S/SGT. HIRAM C. KISER
A.S.N. 33647511
U.S. ARMY

(CENSOR'S STAMP)   SEE INSTRUCTION NO. 2   (Sender's complete address above)

(Moosburg) STALAG VII A
5/6/45

DEAREST MOM, DAD, GRAMP & SIS,
    JUST A FEW LINES TODAY FROM YOUR SON, NOW
AN X-P.W.), TO LET YOU KNOW THAT WE WERE LIBERA-
TED AND WE ARE ALL O.K.. THE YANKS FROM THE 7TH.
ARMY (14TH. DIV.) ROLLED IN APRIL 29TH. AT 1.20 P.M.
"BOY" IT GAVE US QUITE A THRILL WHEN THE OLD "SWASTIKA"
FLAG CAME DOWN AND OLD GLORY BEGIN WAVEING
OVER THE CAMP.
    BY-THE-WAY MOM MY ENGINEER AND I ARE
LIVING TO-GETHER HERE AND JIM CROW & KIPPER
ARE ALSO HERE. JIM, WAS SHOT DOWN IN FEB.
SO WE ARE ALL GRADUALLY GETTING TOGETHER
AGAIN. JIM TOLD ME THAT SIS WAS A LT.
IN THE ARMY AND BOY YOU COULD HAVE
KNOCKED ME OVER WITH A STRAW. WELL I'LL
SIGN OFF FOR TODAY AND I'M HOPING TO BE
ON MY WAY BACK TO THE STATES SOON.
                    LOTS OF LOVE TO ALL, BUD

HAVE YOU FILLED IN COMPLETE
ADDRESS AT TOP?

REPLY BY
V·····MAIL

HAVE YOU FILLED IN COMPLETE
ADDRESS AT TOP?

18

V-mail letter from H.C.
to his family. This
mail service was
provided by the
military to expedite
communication.
During World War
II, members of the
armed forces
were also allowed
free postal delivery under
the franking privilege. This
letter was written by H.C. just days
after liberation of Stalag VIIA in Moosburg.

FROM: S/SGT. HIRAM C. KISER
ASN 33647511
U.S. ARMY

V·····MAIL

FREE
SEE
INSTRUCTION
NO. 2

TO:
MRS. H.C. KISER
ROUTE #2
ABINGDON, VA.

2153

CENSOR

Winters. When the Italian pulled back up to his house, he was still frightened. The Germans would have killed both him and Winters.

Jim Crow was back at base in Foggia, Italy. About a month after most of the *Pretty Gertie* crew had been shot down on the new plane, Jim saw an old man come walking in using a walking cane. The guards checked him. He wasn't in uniform and had grown a beard. It was Winters. He had lost a lot of weight, but he made it back.

At Camp Lucky Strike, H.C. was stripped of all his clothes and given new everything. He refused to give up his baseball glove, spoon, Bible, or jacket. They really fussed about the jacket; it was covered in lice. It had served as his blanket and a wrap for his Bible and glove. He wouldn't get rid of it, so they deloused it, and he carried that coat around until it dried. He left there on a Henry J. Kaiser Liberty ship, called the U.S.S. *Grant*. The ship took them across the English Channel and stopped at Southampton in England for a few days, before beginning the long stretch back across the Atlantic. The ship sailed into the New York harbor; the POWs were so excited when they first saw land. When they saw the Statue of Liberty standing there, they all went running to the side of the ship. It was a monument to all they had been through. Everyone was weeping. Freedom, what a beautiful sight! H.C. began praising the Lord for his freedom, for his life.

He was taken to Camp Kilmer in New Jersey. He stayed there for a while and was taught how to eat again. The Army Air Corp let him come home for a 60 day leave. After that time, all of the POW airmen were taken to the Gulf Stream Hospital in Miami Beach. H.C. lost touch with all of his friends while he was there. The Army Air Corps called each POW in and showed them a map of all the Air Corps bases in the United States. They gave them 30 minutes to decide where they wanted to go. H.C. thought anywhere in Tennessee would be closest to home and chose Smyrna Air Base in Nashville. Greenville would have been closer, but he didn't realize it at the time. The Air Corps wanted the men to appear more human before they returned to civilian life. Each POW had enough points to come out of the army, but the Air Corps wanted each man to have an adjustment time before he came straight out into civilian life.

H.C. hitchhiked home about every weekend. One weekend H.C. had left Nashville for a home visit and was in Knoxville waiting to get on the bus to come back to Bristol. There was a huge crowd, and he knew they couldn't all make this bus. The bus driver wanted all of the service men and their wives to come up first. H.C. started forward with his ticket. A very attractive lady came up and asked him, "Sergeant, can I be your wife long enough to get on that bus?" H.C. said, "Yes." He went on the bus first and the driver punched his ticket. The woman had a long ticket to Los Angeles. The bus driver was punching her ticket, and H.C. sat down watching the crowd.

The woman came and just plunked down beside him. She told him how kind he was and started to make advances toward him. She said that she was a nurse. She had on a beautiful silk dress, and he told her he didn't believe she was a nurse. She said her husband had been killed in the war. When the bus stopped in Morristown, the woman bought his lunch. When the bus arrived in Bristol, they both got off the bus and the woman propositioned H.C. saying, "I haven't been with a man in a long time, and you haven't been with a woman." H.C. said, "I was so infatuated that I told her, 'Yes.' I will never forget it. I watched her go into the ladies' room, and I took out down a back alley and got to the highway to hitchhike. I caught a cab and came home. It cost me seven dollars. I just started praying, 'Lord, how could I do that to You and my mother?' I had only begun to realize how weak we are. How weak all people are."

Chapter 12

COMING HOME

*Praise be to the Lord, to
God our Savior, who daily bears
our burdens.*

(PSALM 68:19, NIV)

The Army Air Force sent a telegram to H.C.'s family in Abingdon that he had been liberated, was still alive, and would be returning home soon. The telegram came to the Red Cross office and a friend of the family, Emily Barrow, rode her bicycle from town to his parents' house to tell his family personally. He also found out that she had personally delivered the telegram to his parents and grandfather, Elihu, that his plane had been shot down and that he was listed as Missing In Action. She was a small, slender lady and so full of compassion. His mother told H.C. that his grandfather was standing in his garden when he saw Miss Barrow coming toward him; he had started to cry. He thought she was coming to tell him how H.C. had been killed. When she told him he was alive and well, he cried even harder. His mother and dad went immediately to Kingsport where his sister Ann was working to tell her the good news. She was also in the military, serving in the Army Nurse Corps. When H.C. arrived at Smyrna, his mother and dad and his sister Ann came to visit with him for the weekend. It was a great time of rejoicing and reunion.

H.C. was discharged from Maxwell Field, Alabama, on October 25, 1945. He had started doing better physically by this time and began gaining weight — but he still looked terrible. He went back to his parents' home and tried to resume a normal life again. He was helping out on the farm as much as he was able and attending Abingdon Baptist Church again. He didn't think that Grace would want anything to do with him.

Ed Sutherland from his church helped him get a job at McClure Motors. H.C. would ride back and forth to work with him. Ed was a great friend to H.C. Jim helped him begin to regain some self-esteem and confidence after being a prisoner. Ed would often tell H.C. to keep trying, not to give up. He would encourage him to keep going each day and not dwell on the past few years of his life. It was very difficult for H.C. to think of all that he had been through, all that he had seen — the starvation, the humiliation, the abuse, the death, the brutality.

H.C. and Grace were married on April 6, 1946. They lived with his parents and grandfather for the first two years. They built their current home located beside his parents' home on the family farm. They had to borrow $7,200, and they thought they would never be out of debt. His grandfather had said, "Now, son, I'm older than you and things are the highest now that they have ever been." He said, "You have a good place right here, your mother and dad don't mind keeping you and Grace." H.C. and Grace were both working, and they wanted their own home. They paid off a ten-year loan in eight years. H.C. loved his grandfather and gives him credit for a firm foundation, but laughingly says, "I believe that was the only bad advice Grandpa ever gave me because things were never any cheaper — everything kept going up and up."

H.C. and Grace had some hard times. The next several years were very difficult for H.C. as he tried to return to a normal life with his mind full of the horror of war, but they were also wonderful years. He and Grace had a daughter Cindy and a son Mike. Even in that time, H.C. knew that the Lord was providing for him and blessing him.

H.C. and Grace have many wonderful memories of the years after H.C. returned home. Their good friends, Ray and Dana Duncan, were rearing their children at the same time. They went to church together and went camping together for entertainment. They were difficult years financially. H.C. had to work hard to make ends meet, but his family never did without anything they needed. The years were even more difficult for H.C emotionally; he was not able to talk about his war experiences. The memories were there, but they were still too painful to share.

Ray was the Fire Chief in Region VI with the Virginia Division of Forestry. He told H.C. that one of the foresters was going to retire soon and that he should apply for the job. Ray said that H.C. should start volunteering for the Forestry Service so that he would have some experience when the time came to actually apply for the job. H.C. would work hard at McClure Motors and then come in and do his farm work. Sometimes he would be dead tired when Ray would call and say, "I've got a fire and I need you to go." He really had to drag on some of those fires, but Ray kept saying, "There are going to be a lot of people wanting that job, and so the more experience you can get, the more it will help you."

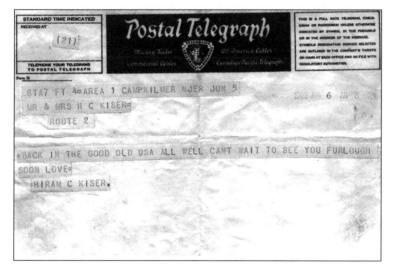

BACK IN THE GOOD OLD USA   ALL WELL   CAN'T WAIT TO SEE YOU   FURLOUGH SOON   LOVE   HIRAM C. KISER

Telegraph from H.C. to his parents after returning to USA, June 6, 1945.

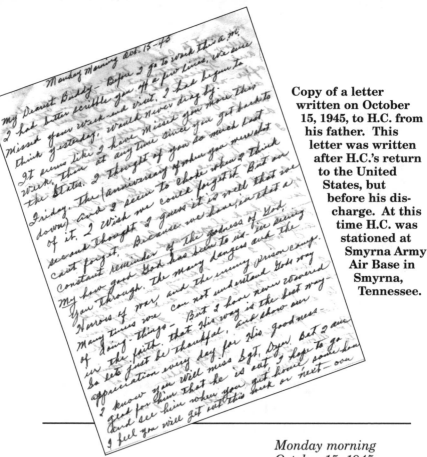

Copy of a letter written on October 15, 1945, to H.C. from his father. This letter was written after H.C.'s return to the United States, but before his discharge. At this time H.C. was stationed at Smyrna Army Air Base in Smyrna, Tennessee.

Monday morning
October 15, 1945

My Dearest Buddy,

Before I go to work this a.m. I had better scribble you off a few lines. We sure missed your weekend visit. I had begun to think yesterday would never drag by.

It seems like I have missed you more this week than at any time since you got back to the States. I thought of you so much last Friday, the anniversary of when you were shot down and I seem to choke when I think of it. I wish we could forget it. But on second thought I guess it is well that we can't forget. Because we have, in that, a constant reminder of the goodness of God. My, how good God has been to us - in seeing you through. The many dangers and the horrors of war and the enemy prison camp. Many times we cannot understand God's way of doing things, but I have never wavered in the faith that His way is the best way. So let's just be thankful and show our appreciation every day for His goodness.

Always,
Daddy

A letter from Mrs. C.C. Black and Mrs. J.W. Woolwine. Mrs. Woolwine was known to H.C. as Granny Woolwine. She was an inspiration to H.C. and this book is dedicated to her loving memory.

Nov. 7, 1945

Dear H.C.

The members of the Missionary Society of your church want me to tell you how glad we are to have you back again. We have missed you a lot and to say we are proud of you and the way you have performed your duties, does not describe our feelings toward you. We are so thankful you have been spared to worship with us again.

The church needs your interest and cooperation, trust you will be present at every service possible.

Very gratefully yours,
Mrs. C.C. Black, President
by Mrs. J.W. Woolwine

95

HEADQUARTERS
ARMY AIR FORCES EASTERN FLYING TRAINING COMMAND
MAXWELL FIELD, ALABAMA

31 October 1945

Mr. Hiram C. Kiser, Jr.
RFD # 2
Abingdon, Virginia

Dear Mr. Kiser:

Upon the occasion of your return to civilian life, I wish to express my personal appreciation for the services you have rendered the Army Air Forces.

Your contribution toward the victory for which we fought, and which, after almost four long and trying years, we so recently won, has earned the undying gratitude of our country.

The personal sacrifices you have made and your unselfish devotion to duty are beyond material repayment. In its stead, a grateful nation offers you its earnest thanks and the opportunity to build, upon the victory you so valiantly helped to achieve, a peace that will bless our country and all mankind.

I hope, in the years to come, you will cherish the associations you have made while a member of the Army Air Forces. Our experiences in a great many respects have been the same. They, and the cause for which we fought, form a bond between us that time will not easily erase.

God speed you home and the best of good fortune in the peaceful years ahead.

Sincerely yours,

Fay R. Upthegrove

FAY R. UPTHEGROVE
Brigadier General, USA
Commanding

A letter written to H.C. by Brigadier General Fay R. Upthegrove after H.C.'s discharge on October 21, 1945, from Maxwell Field, Alabama.

Chapter 13

LEAVING THE WILDERNESS, A BATTLE WITH CANCER

*...for the Lord our God is
He who brought us and our
fathers up out of the land of Egypt,
from the house of bondage, and
who did these great signs in our
sight and preserved us through all
the way in which we went and
among all the peoples through
whose midst we passed.*

(JOSHUA 24:17, NASB)

It was a great career for H.C. — a state job with the Virginia Department of Forestry. As chief forest warden of Washington and Smyth Counties, H.C. fought forest fires, hired workers to man all of the lookout towers, investigated arson incidents, and provided educational services within the schools. H.C. began with the Department of Forestry in March of 1964.

He became a Gideon at about the same time. That was the time that the Gideons could go into the schools. The doors were open and they let them go in and share Christ with all of the young people. He literally put thousands of miles on an old 1965 Chevrolet Nova during this time. He would take annual leave and go into as many schools as he could.

H.C. was also "Smokey the Bear" for the Department of Forestry in this region. He would go into the schools and do presentations as "Smokey." Dr. Jack Garland recently told me that the first time he ever remembered meeting H.C. was as Smokey the Bear. He was then teaching at John Battle High School, and H.C. was going into all of the schools as "Smokey" and as a Gideon. At that time, schools could have religion classes, and H.C. was invited to speak to one of the classes. There was a red-headed, freckled-face boy there named Robert, who was always in a lot of trouble. One night he had been caught doing something and told Mr. Garland that he wanted to change his life, but he didn't know how. Robert told Mr. Garland that he had heard H.C. speak in the Christian club meeting and that he wanted to know Jesus, too. Robert is now a Methodist minister in Lenoir, Tennessee.

H.C. was working hard on the farm, fighting fires, being "Smokey the Bear," and traveling as a Gideon; but in 1974, his health began to fail. He went to a friend who was also a Gideon and who was a medical doctor, Dr. Solomon. He did several biopsies and told H.C. that he had cancer — melanoma cancer, which was incurable. He said that usually a person with this type of cancer would live six months to a year; he had never known a person to live more than a year. H.C. was very bitter and kept asking God, "Why, Lord, why didn't you let me die in the prison camp? Now, I am bringing all of this disgrace and suffering onto my family." His daughter Cindy was a senior at East Tennessee State University, and his son Mike was a senior at John Battle High School. He prayed, "Lord, why couldn't you let me live to see these children graduate before you take me?"

One day at work, he was at a forest fire near Saltville, Virginia. The fire was moving up a ridge; and instead of calling for help, he thought he could put the fire out by himself. He was feeling very low because of his cancer and felt he was out of fellowship with the Lord. He grabbed a fire rake and went to the top of this ridge and started working. The sweat started to pour. He felt his heart pounding, and he knew that he was overdoing it. Just as he had felt the Christmas of 1944, lonely and abandoned, H.C. felt that he wanted to die. He prayed, "Lord, I don't want to be burned, but if I could just go out with this fire, it would be a lot better." H.C. believed it would be easier for his family for him to die in the fire than to prolong his death to cancer.

H.C. was preparing to go back to the hospital for his third operation. Grace, a strong Christian, had prepared their lunch before they were to leave for his appointment. They sat down to eat, and Grace said, "H.C., aren't you going to bless the food?" H.C. replied, "Grace, I don't have anything to thank God for; I am dying with cancer." She began to cry, and H.C. couldn't eat. He went into the bathroom and began to shave. H.C. looked at himself in the mirror. H.C. said, "I knew that I was a Christian ready to die. I also knew that I was out of fellowship with the Lord Jesus; I didn't have faith. I'd had 40 years to grow in faith and the knowledge of Jesus Christ. I said, 'Lord, if I could have an option today, rather than be healed of cancer, I would just have you come back into my life. If I could know your presence in my life like I did in the prison camp, I would rather confess my sins and have you come back into my life and restore my faith and fellowship with you. Lord, I need spiritual healing more than I need physical healing.' Oh, the nature of Jesus! He forgave me, and the tears began to stream down my face. I said, 'Lord, I am going to go and tell Grace what a great meeting you and I have just had here in this bathroom.' As I opened the door — I will never forget — the Lord spoke so clearly and so plainly. He reminded me of the time when I had my hand on the release hatch of the emergency door. He reminded me that I stood in the door with a bundle of tangled parachute, and the Lord had said, 'H.C., I am a God of miracles; and if you will just leap out of this plane in faith, I will show you that I am a God of miracles.' Now, with my hand on the doorknob of our bathroom, the Lord said, 'H.C. when you go out of this door, I want you to begin to praise me because I am not only going to forgive you, but I am going to heal this cancer.' I said, 'Lord, how can I know? How can I be so sure?' The Lord said, 'H.C., I am a God of miracles, trust me like you did in that burning plane.'"

H.C. went back into the kitchen and said, "Grace, God is going to heal me." She asked, "H.C., how can you be so sure." He told her that he wouldn't doubt it for anything in the world. He had just experienced the same presence of the Lord in his life that he had felt all during his time in the prison camp. H.C. told Grace that on Wednesday night, when everyone at church would be praying for him, to call the pastor and tell him he didn't want any more prayers for healing. He wanted prayers of praise and thanksgiving because God had promised his healing.

Soon after this, on a Sunday, following the eleven o'clock service, Grace was talking with Don Moore, the Minister of Music at Abingdon Baptist Church. They were standing in the parking lot outside, and everyone else had left. They were hugging and crying. H.C. asked them why they were upset. Don just hugged him and said, "The Lord is going to take my dear brother," meaning H.C. H.C. suddenly was filled with doubt. He came home that evening and went out on the farm. He had a talk with the Lord and prayed, "Lord, Don is a minister, and Grace is my wife; maybe they have had a revelation from you." H.C. says, "I believe that the Lord will often throw things out in your life to see whom you believe: your wife, a minister, or Him."

If H.C. had listened to the world, he should have been dead long ago. God gave him more than physical healing — He brought him out of the wilderness. H.C. needed much more than the cancer healed. He was walking in a dry and desolate desert of despair. He realized at that moment that he had turned from the Lord. H.C. says, "Maybe I should have died in that prison camp, but Jesus spared my life for His purposes. Whatever obstacles you have in your life, Jesus Christ is greater than any problem you will ever have. I just praise Him. He is God of the past, the present, and the future. He doesn't tell us our weeks and months ahead, but He says as our days are, so will our strength be. I pray that when anyone reads about my life, it will help them to make a decision to turn their lives over to Jesus Christ. The Lord has provided for my every need, and I praise Him for it."

Proverbs 17:17, NASB, says, "A friend loves at all times...." H.C. had a friend like this, a man he worked with named Charlie Christian, a local forest warden in Smyth County. Charlie was a good Christian friend, closer than a brother. H.C. could tell Charlie problems in his life and family that H.C. wouldn't even share with Grace. One day Charlie and H.C. were working a forest fire. H.C. jumped a little creek and felt something tear in his back, and the blood began to pour from his back where skin had been grafted. Dr. Granthum was grafting skin from a place near his ribs onto the cancerous place on his back. He had told H.C. that they had gone down to the rib cage, and there was no more flesh to graft onto his back. The graft was not taking, and the doctor was worried; he said there was nothing else he could do. When Charlie saw the blood pouring from his back, he said, "H.C., you go around sharing with me that God has healed you, but God hasn't healed that cancer. You wouldn't be bleeding if He had." Charlie said, "You even go to churches and share that; I would be afraid to do that!" H.C. said, "Charlie, you know what, you are talking like Satan." H.C. realized that Charlie was really concerned for him. Again, though, H.C. knew that the Lord had healed him, and he stood on that promise.

That was in 1974.

Chapter 14

A FOREST WARDEN

*Whatever you do, do your
work heartily, as for the Lord
rather than for men; knowing
that from the Lord you will receive
the reward of the inheritance.
It is the Lord Christ
whom you serve.*

(COLOSSIANS 3:23,24, NASB)

"There is no use having a job if you don't ask the Lord to help you in carrying out that job." The Lord opened a lot of doors for H.C. in working as a forest warden. H.C. wishes he could say that he had been able to solve all of the arson cases of forest fires while he was there, but he can't. Many of them went unsolved. However, he was able to witness to the people with whom he worked, as well as to the people with whom he came into contact. H.C. said, "I always told the District Forester, Gene Olston, 'Gene, I'm going to tell it like it is.'" He shared Christ at the district meetings with all of the foresters and everyone else who attended. H.C. doesn't miss any opportunity to tell of God's goodness and power.

One morning he prayed, "Lord, do something today to show me we are in this thing together." He was working on a case where a lot of land had been burned because someone had set a small fire, either a camp fire or trying to

H.C. as Chief Forest Warden of Washington and Smyth Counties with the Virginia Division of Forestry in 1978.

burn brush or trash. He had not been able to find any evidence, and he wasn't making much progress. He believed that someone had pulled up into a gap and emptied out ashtrays and the whole field had caught on fire. The fire was on Route 42, four miles east of Rich Valley School. He went up to the elementary school that day to talk with the principal, John Morgan. The principal was busy getting the children into a program, and invited H.C. to go to the cafeteria and get a cup of coffee and a buttered biscuit. As he was sitting in the cafeteria enjoying his breakfast, a lady came up to him and looked at the patch on his shoulder. She said, "You may be the person I need to see." She asked him if he was in charge of forest fires in the area. When he said, "Yes," she said "I've got something to tell you. My son goes to VPI; and one weekend when he came home, he had some <u>Playboy</u> magazines that he didn't want me to see. He emptied all of that stuff out of his car and tried to burn it. It caught the mountain on fire." She said that he was scared to death. She said they wanted to pay the cost of the fire damages if they could. She wanted to know if H.C. could collect the payment right then. H.C. went out to his truck for the fire report, and she wrote a check right there. "They weren't all that easy, but it was such a great example that the Lord was guiding me, and again provided for all of my needs." H.C. could try to do his job, but he knew the Lord could do it better.

One year there was in a particularly bad fire season. H.C. was in Smyth County working on a fire with Charlie. They were about two miles north of Saltville in a little community called Pump Log Hollow. The wind was terrific, and the fire was jumping. It was jumping from one ridge top to another, and they had fire departments on standby. They had fire-fighting crews, bulldozers, and fire lines. H.C. and Charlie told them not to take action until they found a place out-of-danger where they could start trying to contain the fire. H.C. and

Charlie were running down the foothill, and they could see the fire jump from one ridge to the other. H.C. said, "Charlie, what can we do?" H.C. was in charge, and he was supposed to get this fire under control. Charlie said, "I think we ought to pray." They started praying and running down that hill as hard as they could go. They looked up; and finally they had come to a place where the forest ended: it was green, and there were a lot of leaves. They started to construct a fire line. Charlie yelled and said, "H.C., we've got help." He yelled back, "How many, Charlie?" He said, "It's from above." It started raining, and by the time they got back to the fire trucks, water was running down the ditch they had dug and their shoes were full of water. God was in control.

There were many times as a forester that the Lord intervened and saved his life. H.C. said, "I am sure there were many times that He saved me, and I didn't even realize it." One time, though, that H.C. knows the Lord was again at work was when he had to accuse another ranger of being a firebug. Everyone else in the department was very upset with H.C., but he believed this man was setting a lot of fires in order to go out and work them and brag to his girlfriend. He was a boy from a small town in Southwest Virginia. H.C. asked him if he would agree to a polygraph test in Wytheville, Virginia, to settle the matter once and for all. H.C. told him that if he passed the test, he would drop all of the charges and accusations. The boy agreed, and H.C. was to pick him up on a Monday morning and take him to Wytheville for the test. On the Sunday afternoon before the Monday morning appointment, a pastor from a church in the small town where the boy lived called H.C. He said that the Lord had laid on his heart to go and visit this young man and his girlfriend. He said that the Lord kept him there for quite a while. He would think the visit was over, and the Lord would tell him to stay and talk with the boy. The pastor said he stayed, and the boy accepted Christ as his Savior. When he did, he said the boy began to confess to setting the fires and showed him a loaded gun in his drawer. He told him that he had planned to kill Mr. Kiser the next day because he knew he couldn't go take a polygraph and pass it.

Another incident was with "a great big old boy nicknamed 'Baby Doll.'" He was a huge boy who was mentally retarded. He lived up in the mountains with his mother and his sister. H.C. believed that he was starting some fires, and he wanted to go and talk to him. Everyone warned H.C. not to go around him because he would allegedly shoot first and not ask questions. Everyone made fun of Baby Doll and his mother. His mother had a harelip, and Baby Doll was very defensive of her. If anyone stared at her, he would "whip the tar" out of them. H.C. went up to visit with him. H.C. told him that he hadn't come to take him to jail but to fellowship a while with him. He would watch H.C. to see if he was going to stare at his mother. It was a good visit. Later H.C. heard that Baby Doll's mother had died, and he went to her funeral. Baby Doll was so pitiful. H.C. used this opportunity to talk to him about the Lord. He was so upset, and he didn't know how he would get by without his mother. H.C. later heard that Baby Doll had been burned up in his home.

One morning H.C. prayed, "Lord, will this be the morning that I can share you with Johnny!" Johnny worked with the Federal Forest Service. They went to schools together and put on "Smokey the Bear" programs. H.C. had worked with him for years and prayed constantly for him to become a Christian. H.C. knew Johnny was having some problems with his family. On this particular day, they went to Sugar Grove, where they were working several schools in that area. It was close to five o'clock when they finished for the day. Coming back toward Abingdon, there was a beer joint located near Marion on Route 16. Johnny just pulled into that beer joint and motioned for H.C. to pull in. H.C. said, "There he was in his federal truck, and I was in my state truck. Johnny pulls us in to go in and get a cup of coffee!" H.C. said, "Okay," and began to pray, "Lord, isn't this a bad place to try to witness to Johnny?" They went in and were just sitting there drinking coffee; the jukebox was playing and a lot of people were sitting around drinking beer. H.C. and Johnny were sitting over to themselves and Johnny said, "Doggone you, Kiser, why haven't you told me about Jesus? You gave your personal testimony to a friend of mine, and he said I needed to talk to you some-time about what Christ had done in your life." There in the beer joint he asked H.C. to tell him about Jesus. H.C. started sharing with Johnny, and he got very quiet. Johnny said, "Why did you wait so long? My home life is such a mess." He told H.C. about all of the problems he and his wife were having. Johnny said that his life was entirely a life of drinking. He asked H.C. if they were working together the next day. H.C. told him yes and they both went home.

The next morning Johnny was jubilant. He said, "Guess what happened last night; the Lord got after me. I just opened the refrigerator door and threw out the beer I had in there. I got down on my knees at my bed and I gave my heart to Jesus." All H.C. could do was praise the Lord; he was in tears. Years of prayer for Johnny had been answered. Johnny's eyes were glassy and he said, "My wife is fixing lunch today, can you come home with me?" They lived in Marion. Johnny's wife had prepared club steaks for them. They asked H.C. to bless the food. He tried to pray; he was so excited. H.C. felt the Lord moving. They were trying to eat, and Johnny's wife said, "Mr. Kiser, I need Jesus, too. Johnny gave his heart to the Lord, and can you tell me how to become a Christian?" By then, they were all three crying and couldn't even eat the big steaks she had fixed. H.C. had been praying for Johnny for so many years, and the Lord had just moved. H.C. says, "The mills of God grind slowly, but exceedingly fine." We need to recognize God's timing and allow the Holy Spirit to lead us.

Chapter 15

CARRYING
OUT THE COVENANT

*Conduct yourselves with wisdom
toward outsiders, making the most
of the opportunity. Let your
speech always be with grace,
seasoned, as it were, with salt, so
that you may know how you
should respond to each person.*

(COLOSSIANS 4:5,6, NASB)

One day, H.C. was eating lunch at a little restaurant in Damascus, Virginia. He met a man there named Mr. Popp. They were talking and immediately found out that they were both Christians. He was from Damascus Baptist Church. They had a wonderful time of fellowship and began to tell each other about their experiences in Christ. Mr. Popp asked H.C. to come and speak at the brotherhood meeting of his church. He wanted H.C. to give his testimony to them and then again at the eleven o'clock service immediately following. H.C. figured that the men would not want to hear him tell the same story again, so he took notes and prepared a sermon. With his text, he walked up onto the pulpit at the morning service and tried to preach. Mr. Popp began to get very nervous: his face got red, and he was shaking his head. It was a big congregation, and the teenagers were talking and holding hands and several people had gone to sleep. H.C. was stumbling along and couldn't say anything, nothing was making sense.

Suddenly H.C. just stopped, and when he did, the teenagers quit holding hands, and the others woke up and looked up at him. He said, "Folks, I have made a terrible mistake, and I want you to forgive me; the Lord didn't call me to preach. I thought I could preach this morning, but the only thing I know how to do is share Jesus." He began to give his testimony, to share from his heart the love that Jesus had shown and he began to reveal the presence of the Holy Spirit in his life. When they gave the altar call, several people came forward. The Lord said, "H.C., I didn't call you to preach." We all have something in particular that He wants for us; but outside of the realm of what he called us for, we can't do anything. That is a lesson that H.C. will never forget. He watched the quietness come back on Brother Popp's face when he stopped trying to preach and began to share Christ. Then every eye focused on him because that was what the Lord sent him there to do. He was trying to do something outside of His will. H.C. said, "I was called to share Christ. That is the commitment I made when I was waiting on the parachute to open. I said, 'Lord, I will witness every chance I get.' I am sure that is my calling. When I stay in the word and in prayer, the Lord gives me opportunities."

One March, he was driving his state truck and saw a man standing beside an Oldsmobile with the hood up. It was sleeting and very cold. He stopped to pick him up and asked him what kind of trouble he was having. He said, "I'm just hitchhiking — that is not my vehicle. I'll put you at ease. I'm not going to rob you." He started talking with H.C. and asked where he could go to get warm; there was sleet on his clothes. H.C. told him the best place was the jail. He said, "I haven't done anything. I don't want to go to jail." H.C. told him that if he hadn't done anything, then he shouldn't be afraid, and that he would be able to get warm and get something to eat. They stayed at the jail for a while, and then H.C. took him to a restaurant to eat. He told H.C. that his name was David Chamberlain and that he had a son in New York who was sick with pneumonia. He was hitchhiking to get there to his son. H.C. found a lot of discrepancies in what David was telling him. He looked Italian, and his name didn't sound right to H.C. H.C. told him that he believed he was running from the law. H.C. told David that if he truly had a child sick with pneumonia, he would be praying for the child. H.C. said, "I am going to pray that the Lord won't give you any rest until you surrender your life to Jesus." David slammed the truck door, and H.C. gave him a card with his address and told him to let him know when he was willing to make a change.

"Several months went by, and he wrote H.C. a letter. He said, "Mr. Kiser, you were right. I escaped from a work crew in Tennessee, and I was in jail in Knoxville. The reason I told you that my name was David

Chamberlain was that every Sunday a doctor named David Chamberlain would come to visit the jail and stand in line to share Christ with me." He said that he knew that the doctor was very busy, but he always came. He said, "When you picked me up, you continued to share Christ with me. I was under conviction and wanted to give my life to the Lord." He told H.C. that he had turned himself in. H.C. says this story is an example of how the Holy Spirit will tell you what to say when the time comes.

One morning before eight o'clock H.C. was out riding his bicycle. He rode to this restaurant that he often frequented to drink coffee. It seemed as if the Lord said, "H.C. are you wanting to witness this morning?" and he said, "Yes." H.C. usually drank his coffee at the counter, but instead he went over to a booth in the corner. The waitress knew him pretty well and asked why he was sitting way over in the corner. H.C. said, "I'm going to have company." She said, "Who are you expecting?" H.C. said, "I don't know, but I'll have company." A young man came in the restaurant with his arm in a cast. He got a cup of coffee from the counter and came over and spoke, "Mr. Kiser?" H.C. said, "Yes." He said, "You have just had a battle with melanoma cancer?" Again H.C. said, "Yes." He asked if the doctor had given him much hope, and H.C. told him, "No, six months to a year, but God heals." The man said, "I've got the same thing. I'm depressed, and Dr. Granthum said to contact you because you have had the same problem." H.C. witnessed to the young man. The Lord had sent him to talk with H.C., and He told H.C. the man was coming.

Grace was in the church choir for many years and one Wednesday night while she was at practice, H.C. thought of a couple of deacons whom he knew loved the Lord. They were sick, and H.C. thought he needed to visit them. He started to pull out of the parking lot, and the Lord said, "H.C., I want you to go witness to Chuck's father." Chuck was a boy whom H.C. had in the Sunday

School class he taught. H.C. told the Lord, "Lord, I'd rather go talk and fellowship with these great Christian friends of mine than go talk to him." He knew Chuck's father had drinking problems. It seemed as if the Lord would not take "no" for an answer, and He kept telling H.C. to go talk to him. H.C. went to his house and knocked on the door. His wife answered, and she said, "Mr. Kiser, I think it would be a bad time for you to stay here, he's gone right now." H.C. asked her why, and she said, "Well, he got paid today and chances are he will come home drunk, and he will come through that door and he'll kick the furniture, and he may strike me." She got real nervous and she told H.C. he should leave. H.C. knew that God had sent him there and said, "Ma'am, if you'll let me, I would be glad to stay and talk with your husband."

She let him in and within a few minutes a car pulled up and Chuck looked out the door and said, "Here comes Pa, and he's really loaded." Chuck's mother said, "I'm real uneasy, I don't know what he'll do to you, Mr. Kiser." H.C. told her that he needed to stay. He was so sure that God had sent him, and as H.C. says so often, "The Bible tells us that God will never take you where the grace of God can't keep you."

Chuck's father came in; his hair was wild, and his shirttail was hanging out. He walked straight over to H.C. and said, "Kiser, I didn't send for you. Why are you here?" H.C. told him that he wanted to come by and visit with him and that Chuck wanted him to come and talk to him about the Lord. H.C. told him that honestly he hadn't wanted to come, but the Lord had sent him. H.C. said, "I'm His representative, and I have just come to tell you that the Lord loves you and I love you." They went back into a little living room. There was a coffee table with a large family Bible on it which was covered with dust. H.C. asked, "Do you ever read the Bible?" He said, "No, you can tell. It's dusty." H.C. began to share Christ with him and asked, "Can we pray?" He blew the dust off of the Bible and handed it to H.C. H.C. read to him from Romans about how he could be saved. He finally said, "H.C., I really believe the Lord sent you here, I'm sorry that I cursed you and said the things I did to you. I'm sorry. I'm glad that you stayed, and I need to change."

On another occasion, H.C. was working on the farm and saw a friend and neighbor out walking in his field. He turned the tractor off and prayed, "Thank you, Lord, this is an opportunity to witness." Cubie Porter came up and started talking, just making general conversation. H.C. said, "Cubie, you know you've been a good neighbor. We've talked about world problems and farm problems. We've discussed everything in the world, and it has been a blessing in my life to know you. I just want to know what your relationship is with Jesus Christ." Cubie wasn't a Christian at the time, but he later gave his heart to the Lord. H.C. saw Cubie's wife not long ago, and she said, "H.C., I have always loved you and Grace, and your mother and daddy, because my husband Cubie is in Heaven today because all of your lives were such a witness to him."

Another day H.C. had gone to the grocery store and was rolling the buggy out to his car and this huge man came up and said, "Hey, mister, I was in the sixth grade, I believe, down at Hamilton School in Mendota, Virginia, and you told what the Lord did for you when you got in a bad spot, about your prison experience, and how God spoke to you." He said, "When anything goes bad in my life, in my marriage, in my work, in anything, I get strength from what you told." He never even told H.C. his name, and he didn't call H.C. by name. He said, "I was just a little fellow, you wouldn't know it now. I never got away from what you said. Now, when I get into a tight spot, I just remember what the Lord did for you." He wanted to tell H.C. that he appreciated that he had come to his class and that he told him about his life with Jesus. It was just a few moments in the Kroger parking lot, but it was such a blessing to H.C. He says, "The Lord affirms that He loves us and is using our life to witness and plant His seeds."

H.C. was at a Baptist Association meeting and everyone was introducing themselves to each other. H.C. began to feel inferior because each man was reviewing his credentials. When it was H.C.'s turn, he said, "Well, I have been at this church a long time. It's been the biggest part of my life except when my life was interrupted for a short time while I was a prisoner of war." A young man named John Daniels was in the meeting, and he said, "Mr. Kiser was my son's first Sunday School teacher. My life and his life are blessed because of the way H.C. loves Jesus. You couldn't sit in his class without falling in love with Jesus. He had a real bearing on my son's call to the ministry." H.C. won't be puffed up by such praise. He knew, again, that the Lord was affirming His love and encouraging him to share the love of Christ. We all feel inferior at times but as H.C. often says, "Christians are beggars showing other beggars where to find bread."

Chapter 16

THE GREAT COMMISSION, FROM THE OTHER SIDE OF THE WORLD TO THE KITCHEN TABLE

For we are God's workmanship, created in Christ Jesus to do good works, which God prepared in advance for us to do.

(EPHESIANS 2:10, NIV)

"It is 1943, and I am flying into Foggia, Italy, where our plane and crew are to be based. As we fly over Africa, I see a little village with mud-thatched huts carved out in the wilderness. I see men and women, boys and girls, come out and wave at us as we are flying low level in the big B-17. The pilot, Irvin Kipper, calls me on the intercom system. He says, "Hiram, how would you like to some day just drop in on these people — people of a different nationality, and talk to them, try to get to know them and their way of life?" I say, "Kipper, that would be quite a challenge." Then our communication ends, and I pray, "Lord, if I ever have the opportunity to go back to Africa and witness for you, I want to go back."

"It is 1989 and I am flying to Tanzania, Africa, where I and six other men from Abingdon Baptist Church are going to build a church in a small village called Mbingu. As we are flying over Africa, I see a snow-covered Mount Kilamanjaro. As we begin to drop, the pilot tells us to prepare for landing. I see a little village carved out in the wilderness. I see men and women, boys and girls, waving at us. The Lord began to speak to me, and He reminds me of my prayer 46 years earlier. I began to weep. I had a revival in my heart. I knew I was experiencing a miracle. I asked to return to witness, and God was sending me back. I know God is in control, and He answers our prayers in His way and in His timing."

H.C., Bruce Hicks, Don Farmer, Denny Farmer, Jerry Peaks, Ray Duncan, and John Daniels left for Tanzania on February 3, 1989. H.C. had read a lot about Africa before he left, and one of the books said that the African farmers raised a small ear of corn and that they were desperately in need of having someone in agriculture to teach them to grow better corn. H.C. knew a family at Bethel who grew pollinated corn. He got several ears, and he and Grace shelled it and put it in zip-lock bags. They hid it all around in his suitcases.

Grace told H.C. that if anyone had ever gone to jail for taking in illegal goods on a mission trip, he would be the one. On February 5, the seven men flew into Dar-es-salaam, the former capital of Tanzania, and there was a long line at the baggage check. H.C. saw a sign in Swahili and in English that said, "Absolutely No Agriculture Products Will Enter This Country or Leave This Country, Strictly Enforced, Jail or Death." He started sweating, not just because it was hot and humid. The guards were making everyone open their luggage and empty out the contents. H.C. was getting closer and even more nervous. Vestal Blakely, the Southern Baptist Administrator for Housing and Transportation for all of Tanzania. He walked over to H.C. and said, "H.C., have you got a problem?" He said, "Yes, we've all got a problem, I've got good corn here in my suitcase for these people." Vestal said, "Lord, I'm sweating now, didn't you know better?" H.C. told him that Grace had warned him. Vestal knew full-well the seriousness of smuggling agriculture products into the country. He and his wife Carol, though they had signed up to serve in Tanzania for one year, had been there for 27 years.

If you had baseball caps and ballpoint pens, you could go places in Africa. Appalachian Power had given the missionaries some caps, and Vestal had some of the caps and a few pens. The big nationalist guards were about 6'7" and must have weighed about 300 pounds. Vestal went up to them, took out a pen, and stuck it in the pocket of one of the customs guards. He then handed him a baseball cap. The guard was so thrilled he put his cap on, then jerked it off, and put it under a table. Vestal told him, "These men are here to build a church and have a busy schedule, how about letting them go through the side door?" He told them to go ahead.

H.C. and the others stayed at Virginia House in Dar-es-salaam where Add and Jinx Morrow live. Add is the Field Coordinator for the Virginia-Tanzania Partnership. They left on Monday morning, February 6, for Morogoro. In Morogoro, they met Calvin and Vicki Brown, the missionar-

ies with whom they would be working. Calvin is the
Church Development Advisor and Missionary in
Morogoro. Calvin drove them to the church site in
Mbingu, which means "heaven" in Swahili. When they
finally arrived, 12 hours and only 190 miles later, it was
dark, so they set up their tents and lay down to listen to
the enchanting sounds of an African night. They heard
drums beating all during the night and wondered if
there was a ceremony. The next morning they drove to
the village headquarters to meet with the village
Chairman before they could start work on the church.
On the road to the village, they passed the Chairman
and several other nationals walking. Calvin stopped and
asked him about the meeting they were supposed to have
when the Americans arrived, and was told that there
had been a death in his family. The Chairman told them
to go ahead and begin work and they would meet the
next morning. He was walking 30 miles to where his
family was. He didn't have any kind of vehicle, so Calvin
told him he would drive him. Calvin was excited
because he would have the ride there and back to share
Christ with him.

The nationals had to carry the lumber to the church
site before they could begin work. They had stored it at
the pastor's house to keep it from being stolen, especially
the roofing metal. The women nationals carried all of
the lumber and roofing metal balanced on their heads.
The lumber was green and heavy. Every time they
would drive a nail in it, water would squirt out. No two
boards were the same: some were thick and some were
thin. It was very frustrating work. They were going to
build seven trusses. On the first day, they had only
enough lumber to build three. Calvin went looking for
lumber and was able to find some, but not enough to finish the church roof.

Excitement was growing in Mbingu as the completion
of the church building neared. The nationals had taken

H.C. building church pews for Mbingu church in Tanzania.

Abingdon Baptist Church team members taking a break from work in the building of the Mbingu church.

H.C. giving a national a Bible. He told H.C. he felt called to become a minister.

boards and laid them across a fork in a tree and had suspended a piece of steel from the boards. They would beat on the steel with another piece of steel, and it echoed all through the country. It was just like a church bell. The nationals were beginning to gather from the surrounding countryside for the dedication of the church, and a visiting choir was coming from 60 miles away. On Wednesday, before the planned Friday dedication, they ran completely out of building materials. They had plenty of metal roofing but lacked nine rafters to complete the job. Calvin said that when they ran out of something to do, he wanted everyone to go to the headquarters and get down on their knees and ask God for a miracle. He got in his Land Rover and went out in a desperate search for lumber. H.C. began to pray, "Lord, I don't know where the lumber is going to come from, but these people are coming and we are going to dedicate your house of worship." Calvin soon returned, his shoulders were drooping, and he told them that there was no more lumber in the village.

Sometimes the Lord waits until the eleventh hour. Just when it looked hopeless a young African came running up, speaking in Swahili to Calvin. He said, "Sir, I have lumber at my hut." Calvin and H.C. jumped into the Land Rover and started down a path. Calvin was saying that there wasn't even a road there, "We are going by faith, hold on." They got to three little mud huts, and there standing wigwam style against a tree was enough lumber to complete the job. The nationals wouldn't let H.C. carry the big mahogany boards. At the time, H.C. had a long white beard, and the nationals thought he must be very old and unable to lift the boards. There were nine pieces of lumber. H.C. and Calvin were both crying for joy. Calvin told H.C. to climb up onto the Land Rover where he and the women were loading the wood. H.C. looked and from where the wood was standing, one could see the church and the other men working on the roof.

When Jesus accepted the gift of fish and bread from the small boy, he divided two fish and five loaves of bread among 5,000 people and there were 12 baskets left over. Likewise, there was enough lumber to complete the church roof and enough wood left over to build seven pews and a podium. The Lord showed H.C. and the others that He would provide for His Kingdom's work.

The President of Tanzania was supposed to pass through the village, and their visit with the Chairman was delayed again. They finally met with him in his little office three days after they had arrived. All of the men were standing shoulder to shoulder. He had each one of them sign his guest book. They each told who they were and where they were from. H.C. was standing beside Wakemilie, the village pastor. He hugged Wakemilie and said, "This is my brother in Christ; I love you and God bless you. We have come from very far away, a little town called Abingdon, Virginia. God has sent us here to build a church." H.C. wanted to witness to the Chairman and knew that God had given him the boldness to say why they were there. On their passports they did not put that they had come as Christians, but as visitors. H.C. felt that he should share with the Chairman why they were there; they were there as Christ's representatives, not just to visit and admire the beautiful country.

It was a difficult trip in many ways for H.C. and the team. It was an adjustment to learn to boil water and, with the hot temperature and no refrigeration, to drink warm water. It was an adjustment to learn to work with limited tools and wood that had been cut by hand and was uneven. It was an adjustment to work at the slow pace of the nationals instead of the hurried pace in the United States. The nationals were always smiling and were so excited that the team was there and that their church, a building for them to worship in, was

Church progress after "finding" wood rafters. A great excitement had been generated among the workers by God's provision.

Ceremony before leaving the Mbingu community. There was much praying and weeping. Leaving was a very emotional and spiritual time in each man's life.

being built. They were so appreciative of the team and so amazed at their speed and ability.

H.C. had gotten sick on the last day and went back to the headquarters to lie down. A Swahili lady was coming up the steep hill, with perspiration dripping from all over her. She had a big slab of buffalo meat on her head. Flies were swarming all over the meat, her face, in her ears and nostrils. She went over to H.C. and tried to show him with hand signals that she wanted to give him the slab of meat. He tried to tell her to wait until Calvin came back. He tried to explain that they were packing to leave, and they had no way to cook the meat. She had probably walked many miles to give the team the meat as a sign of her great appreciation. H.C. still sounds so remorseful that he had to decline the gift and hurt her feelings. Another man came up in a little while on his bicycle. He had a rooster under his arm. His tribe only had three or four chickens but he wanted to give the team one of them as a sign of his appreciation. Again, H.C. felt very bad about having to decline the gift.

On Friday the village had a grand opening of the church. The nationals had been coming into the village for hours. They were walking around and around the church singing "Amazing Grace" in Swahili. The team was standing on a little hill. H.C. and all of the other men were crying. It was a marvelous experience to see and feel the Spirit and understand each other without speaking the same language. The next morning H.C. walked to the church and looked in to find that most of the nationals had been celebrating and worshiping all night. They had stayed and were asleep on the ground; the whole church was full.

When H.C. returned from Africa, he knew that even though his children were grown and he had retired from the Department of Forestry, the Lord had plenty of "work" for him to do. H.C. often says, "We are not our own, we were bought for a price; if the Lord is calling you to do something, he won't let you go." There is a gleam in H.C.'s eyes when anyone mentions a need. You don't hear him grumble or begin to list all of the negatives or talk about how impossible a situation is. Instead, his excitement is contagious. He tackles every situation with expectation, "Okay, Lord, what are You going to do here?" H.C. will lay his requests before God, and wait in expectation.

After Hurricane Hugo hit South Carolina, H.C. tried to contact Lloyd Jackson, then the Virginia State

Director of Missions in Richmond. He wanted to see if there was anything that he and others of the Lebanon Baptist Association could do to help. Mr. Jackson was already in South Carolina working with the Red Cross food centers. H.C. called the mayor's office in Summerville, South Carolina. Gracie Smith, the secretary there said, "Mr. Kiser, are you going to send about seven men from the Baptist Church? We really need you." She continued, "Water moccasins are everywhere in this low-lying country and when the water recedes, the snakes will still be here. Bring a snakebite kit and a cot and come on down and help us." That was all it took. H.C. began to work on getting a crew there.

A lady from Abingdon Baptist Church, who was very active with the PTA in Washington County, told H.C. that the PTA wanted to do something for a school in South Carolina around Christmas. The Lord led H.C. to Clay Hill Elementary School in Dorchester County, South Carolina. H.C. and Grace went to South Carolina and had lunch with the principal, Jerry Montjoy. Jerry said, "Brother Kiser, I know you want to do something at Christmas time for us at this school, but right now the morale here is so low. We still have trees blocking the playground. Our kids can't go out and play on the swings. If the people of your association want to do anything, I suggest they do it now. What about 30 or 40 turkeys here? We will cook them at our school facilities and we will go out in this little tribal village and feed the Edisto Indians. Many of them don't have transportation, so we will bring them here in vans." H.C. told him that he thought they could get that many turkeys. A few days after H.C. got home, Jerry called and said, "This thing is catching on down here and we will need 50 turkeys." H.C. and Grace put their request before the Lord. About two weeks later they had three pick-up loads of turkeys. The Lord answered their prayers abundantly, 250 turkeys were given to the school and surrounding area.

H.C. and the other men on the Disaster Relief team that went to South Carolina were able to stay at the Baptist College in Charleston. Many volunteers at the Summerville Volunteer Fire Department provided their meals. Mertice Sherwood, a Lutheran volunteer, came in and asked if they would be willing to help on the Edisto Indian Reservation. She had several desperate projects there. She had been working with the chief of the Edisto tribe, Matthew Creel, for many months to try to help the Edisto Indians. H.C. told her that God had led them to Summerville, and they would help in any way that they could. H.C. explained they were bringing turkeys down and wanted to know if they could help in any other way. Mrs. Sherwood took H.C. and Grace to the isolated community of Ridgeville, South Carolina, where the Edisto Indian tribe lived. A downtrodden people, they were living in poverty before the hurricane. Now the community was even more devastated.

One of the homes they repaired was owned by an elderly lady named Susie Evans. Susie was 85 and lived alone. A huge white oak tree about 36 inches in diameter had crashed through her house. She didn't have anywhere else to go. The tree had pinned her in the house. The relief team removed the tree and repaired the roof and walls. They also restored the plumbing and electricity.

H.C. and Grace wanted to visit many of the homes that were to receive the turkeys to see if they would have facilities to cook them. Most homes were without stoves, cooking pots, or electricity. The Piggly Wiggly grocery store in Summerville volunteered to cook the turkeys and make sure they were delivered. They were visiting many of the homes of the Edisto tribe and Mertice introduced H.C. to the Kiser Johnson family, a family that she had been working with for many months. He went into their house and could see the sky through the roof. The sheetrock had fallen from the walls, mattresses were

Masonry students from the William Neff Vacational School in Washington County volunteering to build a home for the Johnson family after the destruction of Hurricane Hugo in South Carolina

standing against the walls to dry, and nails were driven into the walls to hang clothes on. The family was in a desperate situation. H.C. asked if he could see the kitchen; they did have a stove, but didn't have anything to cook in or with. H.C. came back to Abingdon with the Johnson family on his heart. He knew that if any home needed renovation, theirs did.

H.C. prayed that God would make a way to help the family. He spoke at Sinking Springs Presbyterian Church about the conditions the Johnson family were living in and all of the devastation in the community. Before he left, one lady gave H.C. a $20 bill and said, "That is for a new house for the Johnsons." H.C. was hesitant about taking her money and told her he didn't know if they would be able to build a house, but he would use it to buy a turkey. She said, "Turkey nothing — that money is for the construction of a house." She had given all that she was able to give and had made a sacrifice by giving $20. Filled with excitment she felt that the Johnson home was as much hers as it was anyone's. She often called H.C. and asked, "How is my house coming for the Johnson family?"

H.C. went to the Lebanon Baptist Association meeting to give a report on conditions in South Carolina and asked for help for the Johnson family. Each church within the

Progress on the Johnson home in South Carolina.

H.C. presenting a key for the home built by volunteers to the Kiser Johnson family on the Edisto Indian Reservation near Ridgeville, South Carolina.

Association pledged $200. Jerry Owens, the masonry instructor at the Washington County Neff Center, heard about the project. He wanted to help and asked, "Would you let a Presbyterian brother go down there with you? I've got some good masonry students. They had never seen such poverty." H.C. talked to the principal, Mrs. Norma Keesee, and Dr. George Stainback, the school superintendent. They were both a little hesitant, but H.C. told them that the project was not associated with a church; it was just a group of people who wanted to share the love of Jesus and help out their fellowman. Dr. Stainback had agreed if H.C. could ensure that the boys would have a good place for lodging and good food. He felt it would be a great opportunity for the boys: they would gain valuable experience in masonry and even more valuable experience as they saw, firsthand, the destruction of the hurricane and the reality of poverty.

H.C. and Grace along with Jerry and his wife began to pray and search for a place for the boys to stay in Ridgeville. They called every church and organization in the area and were not able to find any place to house the masonry class. There was only one number that they had not called, the Pine Grove Baptist Church, Number Two. When H.C. realized that there was a second Pine Grove Church, he called the number. The pastor's wife answered and said, "Sure, we've got a place. We have a big new facility. Why haven't you called us earlier? This is an answer to our prayers. We want you here." Without any hesitation, she had given them a place to stay and said a refrigerator would be stocked with food.

H.C. went to Summerville to begin gathering supplies. He went into a hardware store there and the store clerk asked him why he was there. H.C. told him that there were several volunteers coming from Washington County to help, and they needed a hardware store where they could buy supplies at wholesale prices. He told H.C. that the mayor of the town owned the store and to go see him. H.C. visited Mayor Verlin Myers who said, "Kiser, anything we have that you need will be wholesale." That was the beginning of many open doors to provide materials for the Johnson family's house.

At home, H.C. called a sawmill in Dunganon, Virginia, and asked for 30 pieces of wafer board. The lady who answered the phone told him that they were bombarded with requests like that, but they could drive over and talk to the owner. H.C. and Marion Dugger drove over. On the way, Marion said, "H.C., don't you think we ought to stop and pray about this?" H.C. said, "Marion, the Lord has already provided; but if you want to, we will stop and pray." When they pulled up, the lady that H.C. had talked to on the phone said, "I bet you are Mr. Kiser from Washington County, and you came to get the wafer board. We are going to let you have it." H.C. just said, "Praise the Lord." The sawmill gave them 31 pieces.

H.C. called Berry Builders and asked for 2 x 4's — they were more than willing to give. He then contacted Warren McCray at Abingdon Tile and said, "We are going to South Carolina as Christian people building a home for an Indian family in dire need. Their home was destroyed by the hurricane, and they are still trying to live in it." Abingdon Tile them $500 worth of linoleum, enough for the whole house. H.C. asked Elbert Umbarger if he could drive them and haul their supplies. Elbert told the team that he couldn't go but they could use his truck, and he gave them $200 for gas. Washington County Social Services volunteered the use of their van to help transport the Disaster Team, building materials, and turkeys. It was definitely a community effort.

In South Carolina the pastor of Pine Grove Baptist Church, Number Two, David Verones, was the fire chief of the Charleston Fire Department. He contacted the local Ridgeville fire station which volunteered to use the destroyed house for practice. They would burn down the old house and clean the area. Other volunteers were going to dig the footing. When H.C. and the masonry students arrived to begin laying block, the concrete had not been poured. Jerry was frustrated and said, "I knew something was going to happen." H.C. responded, "The Lord is going to provide; we'll get that concrete poured." H.C. got on the phone, again, and called a business in Charleston to deliver the concrete. They said, "Why should we bring concrete from Charleston to that swampy Indian village when we can sell every yard we make right here in Charleston?" H.C. said, "I'll give you a good reason. There are 20 volunteers here, and we are going to build this house for

free. The Lord sent us here. If we donate our time, why
can't you bring the concrete?" The man simply replied,
"Okay, I'll have it over there." H.C. and the others took
the Neff Center students to see the ocean at the Isle of
Palms, many for the first time. When they got back, the
concrete had been poured.

The materials were there, the people with all of the
skills needed had gathered, and the house began to go
up. One evening after a long day of work, H.C. was at
the Four Holes Indian Organization Headquarters when
the Lebanon Baptist Association secretary called and
said, "H.C., you have spent all of the funds available for
the Johnson house. Don't spend another dime." H.C.
knew they were going to have to shut down. They were
completely out of materials and now completely out of
money. He prayed, "Lord, why did you send us to South
Carolina, hundreds of miles, after dozens of phone calls,
and all of the generous contributions, and now we have
to shut down?" When he and the other volunteers went
to bed that night, H.C. was unable to sleep. He lay
awake tossing and turning, talking to God. He got up
the next morning so burdened that he couldn't eat. Ray
Duncan was the only other person who knew they were
out of money. The other crew members kept asking
what the plans were for the day. They would be leaving
for the Johnson home site soon and would be at the location in 20 minutes. While H.C. was sitting there, pick-
ing at his food, laying his requests before God and
waiting in expectation, a man knocked on the kitchen
door. He was from another church in the area. He said
that he was embarrassed that his church was the closest
one to the home and they had not been by before to help
or give money. He said he felt burdened to come on this
particular morning. He handed H.C. a donation of $500.

H.C. went to a store in St. George to buy supplies,
and the owner and his son began to talk to H.C. The
owner said, "Let me ask you a question — why are you

doing all of this for that bunch of porch monkeys?" H.C. asked, "Why are you calling these people 'porch monkeys?'" The owner said, "All they do is sit on the porch and watch people go by." H.C. was very indignant by now and said, "These people have been driven back into that swamp. Many people have volunteered their time and money to help this family. I don't appreciate you talking about God's people and God's important work that way." Several times the next day, the store owner was seen driving by the house. H.C. returned to the store, but this time the owner was talking to him about the amount of work that had been done. He was amazed at the number of volunteers and how far they had travelled to help. He told H.C. that an anonymous person had called and said to give them a $1000 store credit, no questions asked — whatever they needed. H.C. believes with his whole heart that it was from the owner himself.

As H.C. talks about this project, he is still so thankful and amazed at God's way of providing, at His perfect timing. H.C. said, "We never had a surplus of money or materials, but we always had what we needed. I believe God does this to make us totally reliant on Him. If we wait on Him and trust in Him, He will provide what we need, not what we think we need or when we think we need it."

The Lord has led H.C. in many directions, and H.C. has listened and followed God's leading. H.C. had gone to Clear Creek Bible College in Pineville, Kentucky, to speak to the student body. After the presentation, Dr. Bill Whittaker, the president of the college, gave H.C. and Grace a tour around the campus. They passed by one little house where the guttering was falling off; it was in very bad shape. Dr. Whittaker said, "By the way, that cabin was built in 1950 by volunteers from the Lebanon Baptist Association." That was all it took. H.C. came back home and called Jim Meriwether, the Director of Missions for the Association at that time.

H.C. said, "Jim, you probably don't even know about this, but Grace and I just saw a house built by our Association in 1950; it is ready to fall down, and there is a young family trying to live in it." The roof was leaking; there was a bucket sitting in the floor to catch water. H.C. began to pray, he asked God to provide the workers and the funds. Many volunteers from the Baptist Association, as well as other churches, went and either stayed in the dorms during the week or just drove up and stayed on the weekends. They completely rebuilt the house and added on an extra room.

H.C. has participated in many projects and has always been available and ready to help with any need at the Lord's prompting. One of the most enjoyable and blessed projects he has been a part of was in his own community, Washington County. People, Incorporated, contacted H.C. and asked if they supplied the materials, would he coordinate a crew to build a bathroom for a family in Glade Spring. The family did not have running water and had never had inside bathroom facilities. Thirteen men volunteered and 340 hours of work were provided. The father had cancer and was unable to use the outside bathroom facility. The mother was a very hard worker and helped the men every day in every way she could. They had a child who was ten years old at the time, who had never had a shower before. When the bathroom was completed, the mother told H.C. that her son was so excited he took three showers before Sunday School. H.C. says that he and the other men had worked on many projects and felt they had accomplished a lot in their lives but when they saw how much comfort and joy it had given the family, they believed that putting in the inside bathroom was one of their greatest achievements. H.C. says, "When the Lord is in it, anything is big."

Chapter 17

A LIFE OF CHRISTIAN
SERVANTHOOD

*For this reason I kneel before the Father,
from whom his whole family in heaven
and on earth derives its name. I pray
that out of his glorious riches he may
strengthen you with power through his
Spirit in your inner being, so that Christ
may dwell in your hearts through faith.
And I pray that you, being rooted and
established in love, may have power,
together with all the saints, to grasp how
wide and long and high and deep is the
love of Christ, and to know this love that
surpasses knowledge — that you may be
filled to the measure of all the fullness of
God. Now to him who is able to do
immeasurably more than all we ask or
imagine, according to his power that is at
work within us, to him be glory in the
church and in Christ Jesus throughout
all generations, for ever and ever! Amen.*

(EPHESIANS 3:14-21, NIV)

H.C. stands out in a crowd. He stands out because of the way he treats people. As the poem printed in the beginning of this book so beautifully says, H.C. is often described as a quiet man with a knowing, peaceful smile. It doesn't matter who the person is, what their denomination, race, or political party, H.C. sees people as Jesus wants us to see others — as God's people. H.C. is instantly noticed because he seeks people out; he makes contact with them. Isn't this what Jesus does? H.C. is God's servant. He knows who he is in Christ. He is yielded and still and, at the same time, excited about Jesus. He is the vessel and allows Jesus to do great things in his life. His eyes are focused on Jesus.

Preston Brown recalls when three Amish families moved into Abingdon. Preston is currently the president of the Gideon Association in Abingdon. H.C. approached him about taking New Testaments to the Amish families. When they went to the Holston River where the families had settled, H.C. wanted to stay and work. He was amazed at how hard the Amish worked with so little to work with. They were using handmade tools, nothing electrical to build their homes. It was very cold, and there were many Amish children of all ages running around helping too. When Preston had to leave, H.C. wanted to stay on and arranged for someone else to take him home. Totally involved with helping the families, H.C. had the man take him straight home, forgetting he needed to be dropped off to pick up his truck. Preston says, "Whatever he is doing, he is totally involved and all of the other things don't matter much. He makes everyone feel important; he gives whatever he is doing his complete attention."

Shayne Crenshaw recalls when he first met H.C. Shayne says it was somewhere in the mid-1970s. He was only a young man in his early twenties when H.C. was speaking at Mountain View Baptist Church. H.C. told of experiences and miracles that God had performed in his life during World War II, and Shayne was so

Grace and H.C. (right) with good friends, Dana and Ray Duncan (left) at Abingdon Baptist Church as Ray and H.C. receive Deacon Emeritus plaques.

amazed he said, "This was in my earlier years of striving to know who Jesus is and how to play the church game to make myself look good and feel good. H.C. talked to God as if he was a buddy who was right there listening to him as he prayed in each perilous moment." Fifteen years later Shayne was thrilled to know that the speaker at Yellow Springs United Methodist Church was H.C. Kiser. This time Shayne heard a witness of a God that he knew to be his friend and Savior also. Church was no longer a game for Shayne, but "a place and means of proclaiming glory and praises to Jesus." Shayne said, "Looking back on my spiritual journey, I find that ordinary folk like H.C. have affected my life more than sermons. H.C. is a man of integrity, a silent hero, a mentor for all who look to him from a distance, a true southern gentleman; and more importantly, a servant of the Lord Jesus Christ, and a friend."

Reverend Carl Young of Wartburg, Tennessee, has worked with H.C. on many mission projects. He said,

"H.C. is a man of vision as he reflects back to the past. Brother Kiser has always been an encourager. This is something sensed by those who know him in a special relationship. H.C. will find Christ in any given situation. This was proven over and over as he shared himself for the needs of others." Rev. Young says that H.C.'s testimony as to how God delivered him from his adversaries "is something to remind the rest of us as to whom we belong and why we belong to Christ. They are enough to wake any of us up to the Lord Jesus Christ and how Christ wants to deliver us as He has delivered him."

Reverend Don Moore of Christiansburg, Virginia, who was Minister of Music at Abingdon Baptist Church said, "There has never been a time in the thirty-plus years that I have been acquainted with H.C. that I have known him to say or do anything unbecoming to a Christian; his faith in God is as pure, devout, intense, and total as can be imagined. H.C. Kiser, Jr.'s, life epitomizes the love of God and the art and practice of discipleship."

Tom Deaton met H.C. when he became a Gideon. He says, "I was becoming aware of Christ and I was starting to enjoy the Bible and be hungry for the Bible when I went to the Gideon camp meetings. Men there like H.C., Kirby Smith, and Ray Landcraft were such incredible Christians." Tom recalls a meeting when a young man came to tell the Gideons about the jail ministry. He says H.C. sort of nudged him and said, "We need to look into that." Tom said, "H.C. is receptive to every possible idea if anyone needs help; he will turn to anybody he can grab and say, 'Let's go help them.'"

For many years, H.C. and Tom Deaton went into the county jail once a week to place Gideon New Testaments and visit with the inmates. When they first started going, they were apprehensive. They had many doubts and fears: "What if they were asked hard questions that they couldn't answer? What if they made the inmates angry?" Tom says that one Sunday while they were visiting, he heard a little ruckus between one of the inmates and H.C. When H.C. had approached him, the man had his eyes closed. H.C. had asked him if he wanted a New Testament, the man didn't answer; so H.C. had asked him again. The man suddenly became alert and grabbed H.C. through the bars and pulled him against them. He started yelling, "Why did you interrupt me? I was in a meditating trance!" H.C. apologetically said, "I'm sorry, I didn't mean to interrupt anything. We are here from the Global Gideon Camp. Would you like a New Testament?" The man grumbled and let H.C. go. Tom said they were both a little shook up after that, but they didn't stop going. He said, "That is what tickles me about H.C., he is just like a pup. If he thought he could go and get a word in for Christ, he would do it. It is just the way he is. He is so excited about Christ."

H.C. viewed his workplace as his mission field. When he was with his co-workers or with the public, he never went about proclaiming to know more about his work or Christ, he was just himself, listening to the promptings of Jesus.

Juls and Barbara Wood moved to Abingdon when Juls took a position with the Division of Forestry. He says, "H.C. was much more than a co-worker and Christian friend. He was a marvelous mentor and role model, although he probably didn't even realize it." H.C. had taken Juls and his wife on a tour of Abingdon to help them look for a place to live. Juls recalls that everyone, everywhere, seemed to know who H.C. was. He says that naturally H.C. showed them his church and invited them to visit.

While Juls was with the Division of Forestry, he saw H.C. close many forest-fire cases. He believes that the key to H.C.'s success was that he could make people feel comfortable and get them to talk, and he would just listen. Juls says H.C. would often ask questions to which he already knew the answer. Juls said he himself often

Hiram Clay Kiser, Sr. and Dacy Kiser, photographed in 1981.

fell victim to this before he learned what H.C. was doing. He gives H.C. credit for teaching him to be a better investigator.

Juls specifically recalls one incident in which he was greatly humbled. He says, "We were on our way to investigate a fire scene and H.C. asked me about an old, deserted, tumbledown, wooden building. He seemed like he didn't have a clue what that old building could have been and asked me what it was. After I had evaluated the architecture and judged the age of the building, I told him it was probably an old one-room schoolhouse that had been deserted for many years. Prior to knowing H.C., I would have had the arrogance to feel pretty good about my evaluation and ability to answer the question of this fellow, who just didn't act like he knew very much. However, at this point in our relationship, I at least had the sense to ask him what he thought it was. He quietly informed me that it was a recently abandoned church where he had once spoken as a Gideon. Oh!"

Juls also remembers the time that a temporary employee of the Division of Forestry "borrowed" some money left in the office, and took one of the state cars out for a spin one night. No one knew what had happened at the time and Juls said, "It was a mystery worthy of H.C.

Family reunion on April 6, 1996, at Abingdon Baptist Church to celebrate the fiftieth wedding anniversary of H.C. and Grace. Left to Right: Fred, Kyle, Cindy, Grace, H.C., Evan, Mike, Zan, Austin.

By the time the investigation was over, H.C. had a confession, a conviction, a witnessing opportunity — perhaps a conversion, and the respect and gratitude of the young man who committed the crime — Amazing!"

Juls said, "H.C. is the picture of Christian servanthood. I watched H.C. at church, in the office, on the road, on the fireline, at the homes of suspects and friends, with politicians and convicts, in the fields, and in the jail cells of the county handing out Bibles. Before my three years were over in Abingdon, I had learned to keep quiet around H.C. and just absorb everything I could. I learned much about working with people, serving people, humility, love for the Lord, gratitude, hard work, and living a consistent Christian life."

H.C. has been described in many ways and has been compared to many biblical figures. Jerry Peaks was part of the team that went to Tanzania in 1989. He recalls the 190 miles from Morogoro to Mbingu. Jerry said, "I recall a portion of scripture where Jesus was in a boat with his disciples on the Sea of Galilee during a terrible storm. The disciples were terribly frightened by the experience. Jesus was asleep. I also recall a time in Tanzania when we were racing at breakneck speed down a narrow, bumpy, dangerous road in Tanzania in an old Land Rover loaded down with supplies. We were tense and extremely anxious, and our heads were bumping against the roof. H.C. was asleep. Having the other great Christian men there in Tanzania with me and especially H.C. reminded me constantly that God is always with us."

Bruce Hicks was another member of the Tanzania team. He compares H.C. to Barnabas (which means son of encouragement). Bruce said, "H.C. can bring up a project and all of a sudden you have ten people saying, 'Let me do it.' It is the way he goes about it. When we were working on the cabin at Clear Creek, it probably wouldn't have been finished, but H.C. would keep encouraging us. He would keep us going back each weekend saying, 'Hey, we've got another weekend, we need to go.'"

Jim Johnson was part of a team that went to Summerville, South Carolina, after Hurricane Hugo ravaged the area. Jim said, "H.C. has a compassionate heart and can communicate with anyone, rich or poor." Jim says that when H.C. saw the damage by the hurricane, there was no hesitation. They set to work and were able to accomplish so much with so little means.

Jim recalls the time he spent with H.C. at the Baptist College while they were there. "Each evening, H.C. and I would walk around the beautiful campus and talk about various things that had happened in our lives. During these walks, I realized to a degree how the disciples felt when they walked and talked with Jesus some two thousand years earlier. The wisdom of life and the compassion he has for those less fortunate shines like a bright star in the sky. It is evident that God has used H.C. for

141

the upbuilding of his Kingdom. H.C. has accepted the role that God has given him instead of rejecting it."

Proverbs 10:7 says, "The memory of the righteous is blessed...." As H.C. and I sat and talked for many hours, I was constantly amazed at the details that he could remember more than 50 years to now. H.C. gives his testimony with such enthusiasm. He describes the sounds of the war, the smells of the war, and the heartfelt despair of the war. He called me one afternoon because he had thought of something and wanted to make sure he had told me about it. He was talking about the wonderful worship services they would have in Stalag Luft IV when Padre Jackson came by to visit them. All of a sudden, he started to sing hymns of praise they had sung together. I asked him if the songs were in hymnals and how I could find the words to them. He said, "I've not seen them anywhere, I just know them." Then he sang:

> *Rolled away, rolled away, rolled away,*
> *Every burden of my heart rolled away,*
> *Every sin had to go, beneath the crimson flow,*
> *Rolled away, rolled away, rolled away.*

and

> *The Grand Ole Book, the Grand Ole Book,*
> *You will find a word of comfort everywhere you look,*
> *In sorrow or in pain, His promise is the same,*
> *So keep on believing in the Grand Ole Book.*

I was totally amazed. These words were flowing from his heart as if he sang them every day. They are imprinted on his heart.

H.C. loves to have "church" wherever he is. As I wrote Preston Brown's comments about H.C.'s love and concern for the Amish families, I recall that H.C. and my husband Mike wanted to make sure the Amish families had a dairy cow for the winter. They began to collect

H.C. kneeling in front of the memorial for the allied prisoners that died in Stalag VIIA. The memorial is near Moosburg, Germany, in the prison camp site. Photographed in September 1987.

money and found just the "right" cow to buy. Then came the hard part — getting her across the river. The Amish have a horse-drawn flatbed wagon with steel wheels, and there was no way to get the cow safely across on it. They ended up walking several miles around Holston Mountain, to finally get "Pansy" to her new home. The Amish children had already named her by the time H.C. and Mike delivered her to their barn. They were so excited and grateful. H.C. said they rubbed and patted her like she was the most beautiful animal they had ever seen. H.C. said, "We had church right there; their barn became a sanctuary as we gathered in His name, praising Him for once again providing for the needs of His children."

Not only has H.C. accepted God's calling, but he loves being God's servant. He says the home in South Carolina began with $20 and the cow for the Amish began with $5, "'Every man shall give as he is able,' and every need is met as we unite in Christ's name, allowing Him to use us in His way and in His timing."

H.C. truly lives out the song, "Sanctuary"©. The song says:

> *Lord prepare me to be a sanctuary.*
> *Pure and holy, tried and true,*
> *With thanksgiving, I'll be a living*
> *Sanctuary for You.*

Wherever, whenever, H.C. is the same. He loves the Lord with his body, soul, and spirit. He often says, "Seek the simple faith, long for God."

As the writer in Hebrews 11 says, "And what more shall I say? I've run out of time...." I praise God for the opportunity to share some of the miraculous, wonderful moments of H.C.'s life with you. I could go on and on. I have been blessed far more by the opportunity to put into writing these words of a life of servanthood than I could have ever known. H.C. and I pray you will be as blessed as you read them — To God Be The Glory!

A Note from H.C.

Dear Friends,

In John 14:6, NASB, Jesus says, "I am the way, and the truth, and the life; no one comes to the Father, but through Me." I fear that some of you reading this book may be in a situation similar to mine. I grew up in a Christian home with a Godly family. I felt that being a good person - I had no need to repent and acknowledge myself as a sinner. My grandfather, Elihu Kiser, kept insisting that growing up in a Christian home didn't make me a Christian. He explained to me that I needed to confess my need for the Lord and turn away from sin.

God help us if we try to get to heaven by simply being good. Our good works are as filthy rags in the sight of God. Although salvation is free to us, it cost the Son of God His life. Jesus Christ came to earth and went to the cross to shed His precious blood that we might have eternal life. Romans 10:9, NASB, says, "That if you confess with your mouth Jesus as Lord, and believe in your heart that God raised Him from the dead, you shall be saved."

The Lord may have spoken to you and you believe that you need to confess your sins and invite Jesus Christ into your heart. If you do, here is a suggested prayer you might pray:

Lord Jesus, I want to receive You as my Lord and Savior. I know I am a sinner and I am sorry for my sin. I turn and repent of my sins right now. Thank You for dying of the cross for me and paying the price for my sin. Please come into my heart and life right now. Fill me with Your Holy Spirit. I want to be Your servant. Thank You for forgiving me. Thank You for eternal life. In Jesus' name, I pray. Amen.

In Jesus Name,

H. C. Kiser Jr.

145

If you have accepted Jesus Christ as your Savior as a result of reading this book, I want to share in your joy. I also want to be in prayer for you as you begin your walk with the Lord. Please send me a note to:

CALLED TO BE HIS SERVANT
P. O. Box 1091
Damascus, Virginia 24236

If you would like to order a copy of this book, please send $8.95 plus $2.00 for shipping and handling *per book*. This shipping rate is applicable if ordering one to five books.

Please send check or money order payable to:

CALLED TO BE HIS SERVANT
P. O. Box 1091
Damascus, Virginia, 24236